SPRINGBANK PAPERS

Through the Sun's Eyes

Volume 1

JIM CONLON

Springbank Papers
Through the Sun's Eyes
Volume 1

By Jim Conlon

©2021 Jim Conlon

Published by:
Nicasio Press
Sebastopol, California

All rights reserved. No part of this publication may be reproduced, stored in a retrieval system, or transmitted in any form or by any means (electronic, mechanical, photocopying, recording, or otherwise) without the prior written permission of the author and the publisher.

ISBN: 978-1-7375814-0-6

Dedication

To Trina McCormick, who for more than thirty years—along with her good companions Ursula, Karla, Teresa, and Anita—has welcomed sacred seekers from across the country and around the world who came to Springbank to rest, pray, create, and experience the transformation of consciousness.

Table of Contents

Prologue 2
Through the Sun's Eyes 4
Ode to Sister Theresa's Heart 7
Seminary of My Soul 8
My Divine Milieu 9
Darkness into Light 11
Sacredness 12
Odd to 2020 14
Pandemic Prayer 15
Disaster Ahead 17
Our Way into the Future 18
Truth to Power 19
Springbank Retreat 20
In This Corner, Hope 22
It's All About Story 23
Pulse of the Divine 29
Birthday Liturgy 30
I Call It Home 31
The Call to Oneness 32
Invisible Excursions: A Compass for the Journey 34
My Journey to the Altar 36
Waiting 38
Sign of the Times 40
My Way to God 41
Turning Points on My Journey 43
What Might Have Been 46
Turnaround 47
Birth of Creation 48
May Tomorrow Happen Now 49
My Turning Points 50
May 1964 52

My Ad Sum Moment	53
Laetare Day	54
Passion Day	55
It's Easter! Alleluia!	56
Justice	59
With Your Back to the World	60
Prayer for the World	62
Charity and Love	63
Getting Personal	64
This Clay Jar	65
The Call of Integral Ecology	66
Dreams and Visions	68
Combustion	69
Prayer for Integral Ecology	71
Privilege and Power	72
To Be Transparent	73
Here at Last	74
Echoes	75
God's Dream	76
Just Pray	78
Dynamic Integration	79
Fragile Hope	80
Patience	81
The Tunnel and the Green Door	82
Broken Mirror	84
Pay Attention	86
Transgenetic Cultural Coding	87
A Second Birth	89
Virus Prayer	90
Message to the World	91
Goodbye Joey	92
Listen and Pray	93
Silence	94

Icon of Glory 95
People of the Planet 96
The Quest for a Quantum Theology 97
Almost Persuaded 98
Goodbye 99
My Justice Work 100
Dawn 102
Thank you, John Lewis 103
Silently Waiting 104
From Fragility to Truth 106
My New Assignment 107
How Can This Be? 109
Questions 111
Portals of the Heart 112
In Toronto and Chicago 113
An Uncertain Pilgrim 119
New Year's Day 120
At the Toronto School of Theology 121
Uncertainty 124
Forgiveness 125
Moving Westward 126
Only God Could Know 127
A Song in My Heart 128
Forecast 129
At Holy Names University 130
Sophia Center 132
A Dog's Life 135
Goodbye Teddy 137
Tomorrow 138
A New Era 139
After the Tumult 140
Holy Mystery 141
Wrestling with Mystery 142

How to Create a Context for Cosmic Fulfillment 143
Tangible and True 144
A Love Letter to the Universe 145
Thomas Tells Our Sacred Story 147
The Universe Story: 149
Our Quest for Authentic Spiritual Experience 149
The Call to the True Self 151
Poetry: A Dream on Paper 153
Prayer: An Encounter with Mystery 156
Spiritual Practice: Habits of the Heart 159
Geo-justice 161
Integral Ecology 162
Transgenetic Cosmology 164
The Edge of Our Longing 166
From the Stars to the Street 167
Pondering on the Precipice 169
Becoming Planetary People 171
A New Morning 172
Epilogue: What You Dare to Call Your Life 173
About the Author 175

Springbank Papers

Through the Sun's Eyes

Prologue

When cultural historian and geologian Thomas Berry retired from Fordham University, he established the Riverdale Center for Religious Research.

There, he composed some of his most important work. With the assistance of former students and friends, he wrote essays that reflected his most significant ideas. Among the books that followed were *The Dream of the Earth*; *The Great Work*; *The Universe Story*, which he wrote with Brian Thomas Swimme; and many more.

In a similar yet vastly different way, I have composed programs and reflections at Springbank Retreat in Kingstree, South Carolina, during my retirement years. I am still active in the church and am privileged to be on the staff and conduct programs and rituals based on my current and previous writings.

The topics were created and selected together with Sister Theresa Linehan, Virgie Fincher, Sister Trina McCormick, Sister Anita Braganza, and the team at Springbank. They include the universe story, poetry, Thomas Berry, Teilhard de Chardin, and integral ecology. Through this work, I reflect on the watershed moments that affect all our lives.

I feel a mysterious and incessant invitation. I hope to understand, experience, and give expression to the questions still rumbling in my soul.

So I once again ask the questions that seem to ricochet from the recesses of my life and trickle softly into awareness. I listen to a silent voice and I let its deep and lasting silence cascade into my soul. At times, I listen and seem to hear nothing. I peer into a deep abyss and seem to see nothing. Yet at the same time, I wish to go beyond each instant and discover an invisible guidance.

May I never place a period where God put a question mark. Inspired by each new awareness, may I always cherish the silent and unseen guidance that stretches out before me. This mysterious silence nudges my awareness and calls me forward into life.

Today, now, and tomorrow, I pray for patience so that what is empty and unseen can prompt each precious moment and so that each moment that emerges can enhance the sacredness of life.

In this silence, may I plunge deeply into the experience that I dare to call my divine milieu. It is an experience that explores the actions of God in the world. It is a promise to listen to the wisdom of my heart. During these precarious times, may what arises from the depths of what remains unseen call me forward from the silence of this hidden place.

Today I search for the answer to unbidden questions in my life. I listen to the silent voice that guides my journey and opens the future to surprise. It is a call that is at times imperceptible, an invitation to embark on the sacred waters of my as-yet-unlived life.

Through the Sun's Eyes

I began this project several years ago, when I felt a prompting to reveal and give voice to my journey.

I chose the title because of its double meaning. You could say this is a memoir that is both personal and planetary. It is told through the eyes of the sun and through the eyes of an earthly son.

It is a pastoral story that recounts the events that make up one's life. It tells of the joys and sorrows that remind us there is a time to be born, a time to live, and a time to die.

This story begins, like all stories, 13.4 billion years ago. It was out of a great flaring forth that my story and all our stories began.

Stories guide our lives in unexpected ways. In their telling, they reveal our origins, they tell us where we've come from and they remind us of where we are. They also provide a glimpse of tomorrow.

You and I have gone this way together. We are born into a family, a culture, and a tradition. We have been chosen. This was not our choice, but rather it is a wonderful gift that challenges and reveals the here-and-now circumstances of life.

This is my journey, and in analogous ways, it is everyone's journey as well. Our stories include regret, triumph, and loss. Our lives are filled with ambiguities and replete with revelations.

In each of our lives there are intercessions, turning points and regrets. As we reflect on our journey, we listen deeply and articulate our destiny.

May these pages speak to your heart.

May we celebrate our lives.

May we travel this uncertain path each day.

May our path bring gratitude and inspiration to our lives.

May the days ahead be radiant and reveal the deepest wisdom.

With gratitude and praise, may we join our lives with the ever-unfolding universe.

May we heal what is broken and renew the face of the Earth.

So may it be.

And may we always be enveloped in wonder and surprise.

May we go forward to savor and embrace new life.

Jim Conlon

Ode to Sister Theresa's Heart

I tell you this story,
so you will never again forget
the beauty of your heart.
It is a heart that is open
to the joys and sorrows of the world;
a heart responsive
to the pulse of the planet;
a heart always aware
of racial injustice,
of fires that ravage homes, trees, lives;
a heart sensitive and wise,
healing us in this pandemic plague;
a heart guiding each diabetic soul
into a cheerful, balanced life.
Yes, I tell you this story
of Sr. Theresa's heart
so you never forget
God is good and so is she.

Seminary of My Soul

Today I stopped and embraced
this beautiful and uncertain day.
As the cosmos swirled and unfolded
around its prior patterns,
I listened for the unexpected presence
of our ever-present God.
May this silent, sacred place
become a seminary for my soul,
where I can discover
all that I can be.

Jim Conlon

My Divine Milieu

On this silent holy day,
I feel your grateful guidance
calling out from on high
and also from the depths below.

Embraced by love,
I feel the mystery
and a call to pray,
to follow the compass of my journey.

I wish to follow
an unmarked pathway,
a path that leads to a future
whose directions I do not understand

I pray for guidance
to discover the unknown future
that calls to me daily,
inviting me to be what I am called to be.

SPRINGBANK PAPERS

Jim Conlon

Darkness into Light

Welcome the dark,
let your light shine.
See clearly now,
even dark shadows
brighten your day.
Sink into paradox.

May each day of darkness
enlighten your way.
See each new shadow
bring forth new light.
Turn thorns into love,
darkness into light.

Sacredness

Today I surrender all preconceived ideas of my life, all notions of why I'm here and who I am and what awaits me.

No longer guided by certitude and clarity, I step aside from the static beliefs that have provided guidance for my life. I will trust more firmly in the sense of oneness that encourages me to move toward what I can affirm is true. From this place, I dare to ask and pray to the Sacred One of sacred days that I may be more fully one.

We have entered a new era in our journey.

We are no longer looking back at the time when Christianity had diminishing impact. The believing community endured a period when religion had lost the cosmos and fallen victim to the fracture that separated divinity from the world and reduced its impact on the joys and sorrows of the people.

Today we are in a new time. We have a new understanding of how the divine presence permeates creation into all life. We are able to imagine that every moment of existence is infused with the energy of the divine. We having awaken to the realization that energy and matter are interchangeable realities, and so we are able to confidently embrace both matter and mind.

With this view, we can conclude that all of life is incarnational. Also we are able to reflect back on a worldview that was previously static and stuck. Science teaches us that Earth is no longer the center of the universe; rather, we now know that it rotates around the sun. With this wisdom, we conclude that the universe is alive with divine creative energy.

The challenge presented to us in earlier times separated God and Earth. This is no longer our understanding. We have been convinced that the divine is present in cosmos and Earth. It is an Earth we are now privileged to build.

This vision enables us to view society and church through the lens of compassionate openness and to heal what is broken, as we see God in all things and all things in God.

Odd to 2020

Don't look back,
look ahead.
Welcome each new day,
with a grateful heart.
Life is always
in the beginning.

Embrace the promise
of each new tomorrow.
Give thanks for all
that has been.
Say yes
to what is yet to come.

Now is the time,
dear friends.
Venture forth,
become fresh energy;
offer that energy
to the world of tomorrow.

Jim Conlon

Pandemic Prayer

Dishes are done,
plates put away.
I step into darkness,
light a candle and pray.

This day, immersed in virus,
many lives lost,
I ponder the mystery:
what good, at what cost?

Our prayer time ticks by,
we hear the bowl sing,
then adjourn for the night,
with courage not lost.

Disaster Ahead

Misguided ones
inflate our dangerous times,
marked by diminished accomplishment.
"Of, by and for the people"
no longer holds sway.
Earth is on fire.
I see disaster up ahead.

Now is the time
to look forward and pray.
Allow your broken heart
be open and pray.
Begin again your journey
and grow your soul today.

Our Way into the Future

We all have our particular work in the world. For some, it may be becoming a nurse, a spiritual companion, a homemaker. In that work, we all long for—if we haven't yet found it—a greater destiny and purpose. Sometimes we are able to identify the presence in our lives that is always inviting us to join our work with the larger needs of the world. This divine nudge may call us to respond to the pandemic and the racial injustice that has been so inflamed in the United States in 2020 by our current president.

Jim Conlon

Truth to Power

Power corrupts,
as jeopardy rules the day.
Outrage obscures
all promise of peace.
Abuse and lies
ignite a desperate doubt
across a shattered world.
Yet in each beating heart
bubbles a molecule of hope
as we breathe one more
great amen.

Springbank Retreat

Springbank Retreat is a wondrous, sacred place. Here on eighty acres of pine-oak forest, there is a magic in the air when you drive onto the property. You experience a sense of the sacred with each passing day. You perceive that you are immersed in holy mystery.

As you walk among the flowers, green grass, and live oak trees, you are awash in an ocean of grace that trickles into every grateful crevice and quenches the longing in your soul.

When you enter the sacred space called Springbank, you are enveloped in a place of mystery and wonder. A divine awareness permeates and floods your soul. You have arrived where you belong; you have come home to God.

In This Corner, Hope

Purple rain
washes across the hardwood floor
as shaking people
strive to make their bodies whole.

On this Monday afternoon,
they walk, box and run
to arrest the unraveling
of body, mind and soul.

They shout and play,
cease the tremors in each heart,
come out swinging from the corner,
rain down torrents of hope.

It's All About Story

Welcome to Springbank.

As we begin our journey into the Springbank experience, you are invited to tell your stories of faith, family, culture, and ministry. You are also invited to discover through moments of solitude, relaxation, and rest how to restore and to pray.

Perhaps we can say that Springbank is an opportunity to pray our lives into new ways of reflecting, and through our reflection, to prepare for new ways of action.

For many of us, our programs and formation were shaped through the vision and writings of St. Thomas Aquinas. In the medieval period, St. Thomas was invited to Rome because the scientific work of Aristotle had become a major influence in the West. Aquinas responded to the invitation by composing *Suma Theologica*.

In fact, many seminaries and houses of religious preparation for the ministry have followed a predictable path. In my seminary days, the curriculum went something like this: you studied philosophy for three years (Aristotle), then four years of theology (Thomas Aquinas).

The writings of Henri Bergson and Pierre Teilhard de Chardin have brought our Christian story to a new awakening through the realization of evolutionary science. Unlike the earlier period, when religion and science were at odds with each other, a new synthesis has been formed.

The conflict between religion and science can be traced back to the days of Copernicus and Galileo. A collision between science and religion occurred when Galileo asserted that the Earth goes around the sun, rather than the sun going around the Earth. As a result, Galileo was put in jail, and science and religion entered an era of divorce and dualism.

However, with the insights and writings of Albert Einstein, Henri Bergson, and Teilhard de Chardin, our worldview has been transformed. Evolution has been born into the consciousness of the believing community.

When Edwin Hubble invited Einstein to look at the universe through his telescope, a new understanding was discovered. The universe was understood to be expanding. Based on that realization, there must have been a time when this unfolding began. Through scientific observation, we discovered that the universe is an irreversible sequence of events. In other words, the universe is a story.

With this in mind, and through the work of Teilhard and later Thomas Berry and others, the scientific story was transformed into what we now understand as the sacred story.

We can say that Teilhard developed a cosmic Christology based on science, scripture, and faith in Jesus. We owe a great debt to Teilhard for showing us the dynamic integration between the presence of God and the evolving and expanding universe. His *The Human Phenomenon* is a treatise on the evolutionary story of the universe. For the believing community, this evolutionary worldview evokes faith in God, faith in Earth, and faith in God through Earth.

One of the great phrases that flowed from Teilhard's writing is "the flesh became word," because he believed that God inhabited matter. This gave birth to what we now call the ecological movement—a spirituality fully celebrated here in Springbank.

We see that God became a human, moved by the sacred impulse of love. Our lives were born not so much from an original fault but rather from an original blessing.

Thomas Berry expanded on the writings of Teilhard, and his view of cultural history became a context for viewing the universe as a story. Thomas and cosmologist Brian Swimme articulated it so well in their book *The Universe Story*.

Thomas's prophetic words remain with us today. He wrote about the need for care of the Earth and for ecological sensitivity, saying, "We will go into the future as a single sacred community or we will all perish in the desert." These words have an impact on us here as we engage on the Springbank journey.

The universe story is the master narrative for our times. On our journey, it has displaced the story of Genesis, which remains influential among the believing community of the West. The story of the universe is a story of hope, love, and anticipation.

As Pope Francis so profoundly announced in his encyclical *Laudato Si'*, we are called today to care for our common home. The believing community and each of us are invited to love God, to love our neighbor, and to love creation in and through the Earth.

As we embark on the Springbank sabbatical journey, we are aware that each of our stories—personal, sacred, and hope-filled—are stories of grace and celebration. Each of our stories is now a paragraph in the one seamless story of the universe itself. May each of us as we compose our new chapter in the great story, embrace each moment as a doorway into new beginnings.

As we gather, guided by the protocols designed to protect us from the virus, we are aware that January 6, 2021, was a moment that endangered the future of our planetary community. We are called to be people to heal what is broken and renew the face of the Earth. We imagine that the story we reflect on these days is a liberating story. It is a story of freedom, as we recover from the tragic separation of dualism that deprived us of a sense of the sacred in the presence of the divine in our midst.

It is a time to heal and transform all that stands in the way of beauty and belonging. It is a time to heal the separations between humanity and the divine, between men and women. Our new story makes it possible for us to experience the presence of our loving God.

We come together at Springbank with our own unique gifts, each with our story to tell, each alive with an experience of the divine presence in and through our lives. Yes, it is a time for new beginnings.

We heard the words of Amanda Gorman, who delivered her prophetic and powerful poem at the inauguration of Biden and Harris: "There is always light if only we are brave enough to see it, if only we are brave enough to be it."

At the dawn of a new era in America, we can be moved by the sacred words of the psalmist who wrote, "Weeping may endure for a night, but joy comes in the morning."

I am reminded of a moment some years ago in my home country of Canada. It was Sunday afternoon and I drove out to visit Dorothy Tennyson, the widow of my brother and my favorite baseball coach. I found Dorothy outside walking among the fruit trees.

I asked Dorothy how and what was she doing, she said, "I'm just out here in the backyard growing my soul."

So if a friend back home asks what you are doing in Springbank, you can say, "I am just here amidst eighty acres

of pine trees and trails, reflecting on the great story of the universe and growing my soul."
 Amen.

Jim Conlon

Pulse of the Divine

Alive, alert and wondering,
no longer static and stuck,
immersed in holy mystery,
set my heart on fire.

I feel radiance rising from within,
enveloping a vast ocean of grace,
pulsating to all that was
and is yet to be.

On this day we become pilgrims,
like the host on the altar,
about to be transformed,
we are ready to heal our endangered world.

Birthday Liturgy

Remembering my flaring forth
on this day,
I give great thanks
for the day when I was born.
Memories of the great flaring forth
wash upon my soul.
I rejoice that I was present
when the stars were born.
Today I look back
and rejoice with lasting thanks
to my mother Elizabeth,
the one who gave me life.
With deep gratitude,
I give great thanks
for all that was and is to be.
Amen.

Jim Conlon

I Call It Home

Some call it the planet,
some call it Earth.
I call it home.

A place of beauty and belonging,
a place of joy and jubilation,
a place of divine creative energy.

A world of wonder,
where every creature
celebrates its wild and abundant life.

Deep in my heart
lies a great story,
a story that wants to live.

Shelley has a name for it,
so do Beau, Bailey and Josh.
Brian also has a name for it.

Together we raise our voices and say,
"If we are here for anything at all,
it's to take care of this sacred place,
this land of beauty we call home."

The Call to Oneness

Programs of formation are often influenced by traditional understandings of society and soul. The divine has been understood as distinct from Earth and its people. This separation has created a chasm between God and our lives in the world, between the divine and the sacredness of life.

Many formation programs were predicated on a distinction between supernatural and natural grace. They viewed justice making and our actions in the world as having lesser status.

However, a profound shift in our awareness has emerged in recent years. Today we are beginning to heal the unfortunate sense of separation. The emergence of science and the new cosmology has contributed to this healing shift. We now view the cosmic Christ as present in the whole world.

If we can understand that God is in all things and all things express the presence of the divine, then our spirituality can flow from a new and more integral approach.

People who participate in programs such as the Springbank Retreat find themselves experiencing a new program of formation. This new worldview is often referred to as *panentheism*. Teilhard was an exponent of panentheism, a term well described by medieval mystic Mechtilde of Magdeburg. It provides an opportunity to reinvent our lives and the call to ministry to do whatever needs to be done.

At Springbank, we are able to reinvigorate our body and soul as we prepare to joyfully respond to the call of spirit and a fresh way of practicing ministry in the world. With each passing day, the world is seen as different and new, as a place where beauty shines forth and mystery gives expression to God's other name.

Today we embrace the wisdom and awareness that we cannot turn our backs on the pain of the virus, racial injustice, and the climate changes that ravage our homes and our people. Rather, we are called to bring fresh energy and divine presence into a world longing for sacredness, wonder, and divine depth.

Invisible Excursions: A Compass for the Journey

To engage in invisible excursions is a spiritual practice. Among its characteristics are a keen sensitivity to the promptings of each moment; a capacity to trust one's intuition without being clear about the outcome, and to dream and engage in a variety of acts of creativity that will liberate the imagination; and the capacity to reflect on and enhance the understanding that at the very heart of our existence we are genetically coded for a life of creativity and compassion that will be manifest in a series of events that can make possible a more mutually enhancing world.

My life has been marked by many such invisible excursions. They have been the compass for my inmost self and have energized new directions in my life. Each invisible excursion is a new chapter in the universe story, each growing out of a threshold moment clothed in mystery.

Invisible excursions happen when I awake to each new moment and am responsive to the hour of the unexpected, and find in the events of each day a tabernacle of divine presence. I approach my life with an evolutionary spirit. I have never wanted to see my life mapped out before me. I have sought to view it through the lens of the promptings of the spirit. I have always wanted to be open to the guidance that found expression in the creative energy that arose from the recesses of my soul and the heart of the universe, inviting me into alignment with the needs of our time.

Invisible excursions have a history in the literature of theology, philosophy, psychology, and cultural history. Thomas Merton was referring to that desire for guidance from the depth of the soul when he wrote about the true self—that *point verge* where we are totally vulnerable and transparent before God. Teilhard de Chardin spoke about the divine milieu where we go down into our inmost self and we find the wellspring that we dare to call our life. Carl Jung described the layered dimensions of the human psyche as containing as many galaxies as can be found in the universe itself. Stan Grof said that when we sink below the level of our thoughts, we are able to find a mirror that reflects back not only who we are but our place in the universe. Thomas Berry invited us to take down the shield of our heart, reinvent ourselves, and begin again, guided by a wisdom that resides beyond conscious thought. The French philosopher Jacques Maritain wrote about the preconscious of the spirit, which hovers between the conscious and the unconscious and evokes in us invisible excursions into the future. Theologian John Haught suggested that we should no longer think of God as having a plan, but rather a vision. In *Beauty: The Invisible Embrace*, poet and philosopher John O'Donohue wrote of the hidden, mysterious epiphanies of beauty in our lives that contain our call to heal and bring fresh hope into the world.

I often say that an invisible excursion can be understood as falling in love, whereby all barriers, all defenses, and all separations melt away. We become one with the person, one with the idea, one with the project, one with the Earth, one with the divine. We embrace our true self and are guided to that place in which we can listen with the ear of our heart, and respond to the cry of creation and the needs of our time.

My Journey to the Altar

As I wonder about my life and the many twists and turns that brought me to this place, I ask what factors guided my path and brought me to where I find myself today.

Perhaps the answers lie in the accidents of my early years, of which I have no memory. For four and half years, my mother was ill and unable to take care of me. Or perhaps it was the time I spent with my Aunt Margaret and Clarice that altered my life and made a deep imprint on my soul.

My mother, Elizabeth Bedard, was the daughter of Alexander Bedard and Olive Gravelle. She was raised in a small town in Ontario, Canada. Her French Canadian roots were reflected in her cultural environment. The French Canadian people were conquered by the British on the plains of Abraham. After their defeat to the British army, they lived in French settlements. There, they managed to maintain their language and their culture. My mother was unable to speak any language but French until she started school.

My father traced his ancestral origins to the times of the Druids and Celts. His people were forced to move to Canada to avoid starvation during the potato famine. The new world where they settled was very much like the countryside they left behind.

My early years were an unsettled time in life. Whether I was with my parents or my aunts, I felt homeless. I felt a need to be somewhere else. Today, however, I embrace the dynamics of my unlived and unfinished life.

In elementary and high school, I was shaped by the society of the post-World War II years. The industrial wheels were turning. We lived in the chemical valley of Canada, where Imperial Oil Limited and Polymer Corporation flourished.

As a child of Canada's chemical valley, I was fascinated with chemistry.

I understand now that my life began with the formation of hydrogen and helium almost fourteen billion years ago. In a true sense, I was born out of hydrogen and helium, and my journey evolved into the supernova experience from which the elements of life were born. From this cosmic journey came the formation of rocks and planets.

Following the emergence of rocks, water, flowers, and trees, humanity flourished on Earth. At that amazing moment, self-reflective consciousness was born, and creation became conscious of itself.

Waiting

We remember the day the child was born.
Holy mystery filled the air.
Suddenly there was no distance,
no twoness.
Christmas happened.
Divinity descended on Earth.
Everything is holy.
Nothing lies beyond
the divine embrace.

Jim Conlon

Sign of the Times

Take courage, dear friends,
we are at the edge of new beginnings,
a deeply felt awareness.
Evolution is a sign of the times.

The divine spirit speak to us,
revealing the gospel of life
that continues to rise and fall,
rise and fall again.

At this new instant,
let your spirit speak
now and once again.
Evolution is a sign of the times.

Through the future,
one could say today,
evolution is alive.
Evolution is us.

Jim Conlon

My Way to God

I want to tell you a story. It is the story about my way to God. I was the youngest of three, and our world was the rural landscape of Sombra's ungiving clay. Each Sunday morning, my sister, Mary; brother, Bob; and parents, Richard and Elizabeth, went to St. John the Evangelist, the mission church in Sombra, for the 9:30 a.m. liturgy.

Throughout the week, my father would invite us to kneel as we recited the family rosary. Before bedtime, I knelt at my mother's knee to recite my evening prayer. These practices were the way I addressed the presence and place of God in my life.

As the years passed, my notion of the divine evolved. My days were accompanied by moments of doubt and uncertainty. My mother's death, when I was eighteen, followed by disappointing results in my grade 13 classes (trigonometry and literature) contributed to my depression.

As I grew into my adult years, I encountered psychoanalysis, which proposes that God is simply a projection of the mind, and that the divine will vanish when our projections are resolved. This approach contributed to the alienation that characterized the "God is dead" era. As I heard more about this approach, my world became secular and devoid of the sacred.

Today, I look back over those years and give thanks for how my days unfolded. I feel comfort in the conviction that the God of my childhood is present in every grain of sand and in every flower, person, and place.

The God you cannot see, feel, touch, taste, or smell is fully present in everything you can. It is a divine presence that dwells in the soul of all creation and envelopes all things.

The experience and felt sense of the divine are both elusive and real. When I read, pray, and listen, a quiet and gentle presence infuses my awareness and embraces my soul.

Jim Conlon

Turning Points on My Journey

During these treacherous times, my questions are similar to yours, as all of us venture forth in uncertainty. My questions leave a longing in my heart. They are my pursuit of meaning, direction, and depth.

I received a message today from my friend. The news was direct and unvarnished. A good friend of many years, Martin, passed away. He lived a good and generous life. With the love of his life, his wife, he shared the adoption of two amazing people, each born in the tumult of Central America. They now live in Canada, their adopted home. Each of these good people is on a journey in pursuit of meaning and purpose.

Somewhere in our souls, we wrestle with relentless curiosity about who we are and what life means. I'm here to come to terms with these questions in my heart.

In my early years, I felt driven to find the place Dr. Martin Luther King, Jr., spoke of when he proclaimed at the culmination of his journey, "Free at last! Thank God Almighty, I am free at last." It was then that I began to experience what I now call a longing for intimacy.

As the years passed, I felt the calling to experience depth and meaning every day. I began to ponder with curiosity the road ahead. Today I feel the calling as a stirring in my heart, a felt sense of wonder rising from the wrestling in my heart.

I look back now to the years when I was young. Those days were times of accomplishment, anxiety, disappointment, and loss. Yet I always felt committed to protecting and advancing the needs of the underdog—those who had been disadvantaged by history, heritage, and story.

When I think of my early days full of turmoil and disorientation, I recall the passing of my parents. My mother had surgery for cancer during my teenage years. One day when I got off the school bus that was delivering me home from Wallaceburg District High School, my Aunt Margaret met me at the bus. She had a worried look on her face. She told me that the doctor said my mother did not have much longer to live.

I was too young to grasp the full significance of that moment. In the days that followed, I felt compelled to tell my mother that I would be all right and that my future was bright and promising. I would go to Queens University in Kingston, Ontario, and enroll in a program for chemical engineers. I would join my brother and sister, who were both studying and preparing for their future. Mary was studying Latin and French and planned to become a specialist in money and banking. My brother planned to become a civil engineer, following the legacy of our uncles Harry and Ed.

The plan I presented to my mother did not take place as I explained it to her that day. After her passing, I lived with my father and attended high school. I often visited my mother's two sisters, Margaret and Clarice, on the weekends. At the end of that year, I opened an envelope from the Ontario Department of Education that contained the results of my exams. I was saddened and astonished to discover I had failed both trigonometry and literature. That meant I was not eligible to go to Queens and be with my brother and sister.

As a result, I stayed at home with my father. I prepared his evening meals and kept house for both of us. During that year, I was alone a lot and often depressed. That fall, I sought employment in a variety of places and was hired for seasonal work at a Canadian sugar factory. My work was in the quality control laboratory.

When the season ended, I was once again unemployed and in need of another position. I started taking two classes by correspondence and was hired in a low-level position with the Toronto Dominion Bank. I had to handle paperwork from other branches in the city of Sarnia and I met many people who came to process their funds.

Later that spring, I was fortunate to secure a position with Imperial Oil Limited Research Laboratory. The compensation was generous and the work interested me. I felt I had found the career for my future. In the fall, I enrolled at Assumption University of Windsor, with a major in chemistry.

What Might Have Been

Contemplate the turning points,
ponder for a moment
the way it might have been.
Distance can provide wisdom,
sometimes amazement or surprise.
So say thanks to the unknown,
embrace what's present now.
Dismiss what might have been.

Turnaround

Chaos stumbles in the dark.
Clarity and vision fade.
Yet, amidst the stumbles
a guiding light appears,
illumination, some would say,
showing a better way.
St. Hildegard of Bingen
shared her way to God.
Now it's our turn
to pray for a turnaround.

Birth of Creation

As I reach for a newly vibrant awareness of the
    divine,
I become aware that within my spirit
resides the ever-present God.

Outside and all around me,
I feel the pulsating presence
of our ever-loving God.

I awaken to a fresh awareness
of the ever-wondrous one,
who heals, purifies, and protects.

The transcendent divine
calls forth the voice
that cocreates the world.

On this seemingly unexpected day,
I again stop, pray and listen.
My awareness widens.

In the silence and emptiness of each moment,
I am suspended in the floating abyss
from which all of creation is once again born.

May Tomorrow Happen Now

Today I ponder this question:
What does it mean to look forward
to an event that has not yet appeared?
I feel a deep conviction
that I must commit to and complete
whatever I feel impelled to accomplish,
whether it makes sense or not.
My life is guided by an impulse
hovering in the preconscious of my spirit.
An invisible presence calls out to me
and invites my attention and response.
That urgency remains present
and pulsating in my heart.
I ask for a response
to the unbidden questions in my life
as I strive to listen to the silent voice
that guides my journey and opens to surprise.
May I always celebrate its divine nudges.

My Turning Points

On a spring day, my brother and I and our first cousin, Fr. Bob Bedard, were sitting in the living room of my Aunt Margaret's home. The home was called Eden Villa.

As we enjoyed freshly baked raisin buns prepared by Aunt Margaret, our attention turned to Fr. Bob. He was in the area because he was going to preside at the wedding of relatives in the town of Sarnia. Sarnia was the home of Imperial Oil Limited. My uncle Edward Bedard had been mayor of this city.

Fr. Bob asked us, "Has either of you ever considered becoming a priest?"

As his words tumbled across Aunt Margaret's living room, I gazed at the St. Claire River, which was shining brightly in the afternoon sun. The first to answer Fr. Bob's question was my brother Bob. His response was clear and decisive: "I'm already in the engineering program in Assumption University in Windsor. I want to follow in the shoes of Uncle Harry and Uncle Ed and the father of the bride."

My response, however, was uncertain. I was both surprised by the question and at the same time unclear about my response. After failing my grade 13 exam, I was taking two courses by correspondence. I was planning to study chemistry at Assumption University. This choice was prompted by my affection for the subject of chemistry and my admiration for my high school chemistry teacher, Mr. Balkwell. It seemed at the time the best option for my future.

However, Fr. Bob's question remained in my heart, even as I continued to study chemistry and complete the requirements for a bachelor of science. After graduating with a degree in chemistry, I entered St. Peter's seminary to study philosophy and theology and was ordained in 1964.

May 1964

The sun rose that morning
in May of '64.
It was a special day for each of us,
our ordination day.

We knelt before the bishop,
said our Ad Sum
when our name was called,
announcing that we were there.

Thus began my journey of now 56 years
from parish to classroom to street.
Today I wake at Springbank,
here among the trees.

It has been a sometimes rocky road,
an uncertain path.
Today I give thanks on this Pentecost eve
and thank God I am here.

My Ad Sum Moment

May 30, 1964, was a day of great significance. It was the day of my ordination. I woke from a restless sleep in my room at St. Peter Seminary in London, Canada. Following a modest breakfast, I joined my classmates as we drove across the city to St. Peter's Basilica for the 11 a.m. celebration. As we vested in the sacristy, we joined the procession to prepare for the ordination liturgy. Those present included my family—my father, Richard; my sister, Mary; and my brother, Robert—as well as my friends.

The cathedral grew silent as the Most Reverend Gerald Emmet Carter and the seminary rector Msgr. AP Mahoney began the service. The rector called the names of the candidates who were present.

When he called my name, James Alexander Conlon, I responded "Ad Sum," or "present!"

The ceremony continued as the bishop placed his hands on my head as a gesture of ordination. The anointing of the hands of the newly ordained was followed by the Eucharistic concelebration of the bread and wine. When the ceremony concluded, the newly ordained approached the altar railing to receive the blessing.

Fifty-six years later, I look back at this defining moment in my life. I have arrived at my eighty-fourth birthday and I anticipate what is next on my journey.

Laetare Day

On this silent joyful day,
I feel divine presence
permeate my soul.
May I be soaked in wonder,
as with great joy,
the universe sings,
"All is holy now."
All is holy—even the smallest being
and the cosmos herself.
Together we pray,
for today is Laetare Day

Jim Conlon

Passion Day

We go outside,
bless the palms,
join the procession,
enter the chapel.

Once again I ask,
"What is this day?
Is it about misery
and pain?"

Now I awaken and say,
"It is about love,
love for you
and all of God's people."

As together we pray,
love is our passion,
love on this day.

It's Easter! Alleluia!

Across the mountains,
beyond the seas,
the Cosmic Christ appears
on this Easter day.

We remember the great story
in our hearts,
a story of wisdom,
of depth and amazement.

We give thanks for this day
for sunshine and flowers and friends.
We ponder the meaning of Easter
on this trembling pandemic day.

We are grateful for each other,
surrounded by so much illness and death.
The presence of the Cosmic One
wraps us in memories of another time.

My mind goes back
to Good Fridays as a child.
In our Canadian village, it always rained
as my father planted potatoes.

My parents brought us inside
to pray the rosary.
I imagined how Earth shook
the moment Jesus died.

Jim Conlon

Today at Springbank,
we hear the Passion Journey,
the way of the cross
now nourished by the Eucharist.

We sink into the solitude of the forest,
dispel the darkness,
celebrate the presence of the Cosmic Christ,
the one who is both glorious and wounded.

As the sun sets
on this palmetto place,
we go outside into darkness
and light the Paschal candle.

We share the fire,
dispel the dark of the world.
Then we join the procession, enter the chapel and
proclaim the church's greatest hymn, the Exsultet.

We say yes to the cosmos,
feel empowered to face the challenges of tomorrow,
to once again encounter
what is dying and what is being born.

Through this sacred celebration,
the great story is told,
a story of beauty,
brokenness and Easter love.

Today the Cosmic Christ
transcends the confines of space and time.

The whole universe is filled with divine creative
    energy,
every place is a place to find God.

This morning, we don't go to church to find God;
rather, we celebrate God in all things and all things
    in God.
We proclaim a joyful chorus
and remember the wounds of virus and death.

We offer gratitude to those who toil to save lives,
who risk their own future to tend to the afflicted.
This Easter Sunday, we remember our journey
of seder, Stations of the Cross, the Exsultet and vigil.

We realize God is not just here,
God is everywhere,
as this sacred moment,
we burst into song!

Justice

Justice and its practice have interested me over many years. Meister Eckhart tells us, "The person who understands what I have to say about justice understands everything I have to say."

In recent years, I have explored the notion that beauty is a comprehensive and compassionate expression for harmony balance and enduring peace.

To proclaim that justice flows out of a cosmic dynamic, we could say that justice is a manifestation of cosmic integrity.

Justice has frequently been relegated to obligation and guilt. For most of my life, I felt called to bring about a liberating possibility, an ability to act that flows from passion, love, risk, and freedom.

When I reflect on justice, I visualize what it means to be delivered to myself, to walk through life guided and empowered to be the person I am meant to be, and to invite others to do the same.

I reflect on the call to bring beauty into the world and contribute to the unfolding dynamics of the universe, as I am increasingly aware that my modest efforts will contribute to the well-being of people and all creation.

With Your Back to the World

You can't do geo-justice
with your back to gun violence,
to racial disparity,
to planetary devastation.

You can't do love
with your back to the world,
when you're awash in anger,
prejudice and pain.

Today we look forward.
We turn toward the world,
toward a time of balance,
of harmony and peace.

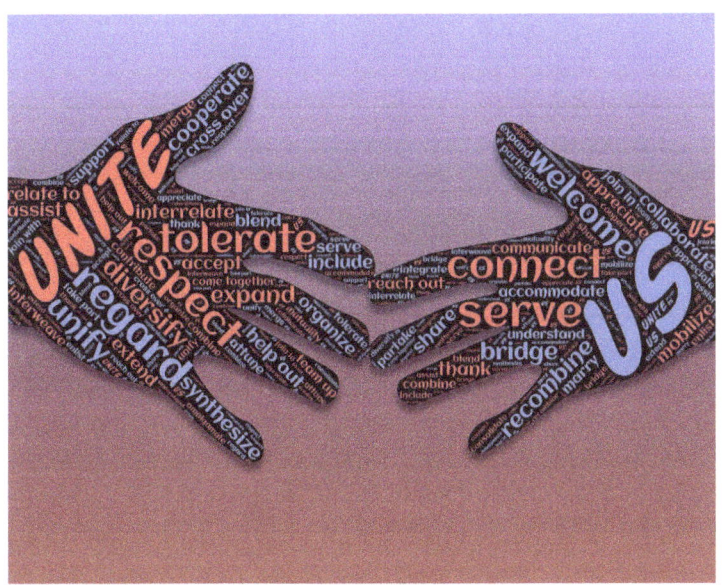

Prayer for the World

What can I say to the world,
blinded by light,
shining to illuminate the darkness,
the darkness of my soul?

Is this not a joyful moment?
Joe Bidden is now our president.
He knows well heartbreak and loss.
Today he invites us to gather and heal,
to knit together our unraveled sleeve of care.

Today we blossom forth
with Kamala as our companion,
as together we pray,
"May we be holy, make us one again."

Let hope and gratitude flourish
as we return to the land of beauty
and pray the words of JFK:
"Ask not what your country can do for you,
ask what you can do for country."

Yes, dear God, make us one again.

Charity and Love

Years ago, a Latin chant made an indelible imprint on my soul. These were the words: *Ubi caritas et amor Deus ibi est.* "Wherever charity and love abide, God is there." As I reflect on these words, I yearn to give expression to the divine impulse in my soul, to what I call my divine luminosity.

Love is like a plasma for my soul. It graces me to take a deep dive into each new moment, a plunge into each bottomless abyss. A magnetic intuition calls me downward and forward into a vast awareness.

Our human capacity for charity and love is deepened through God's invitation to embrace what is and also what is not yet. Each grace-filled instant thunders into consciousness and is empowered from within.

Getting Personal

Experience the updraft.
Even as the virus
infuses planet home,
a new power erupts,
thoughts of Jesus burst into focus.

Shackles of abstraction fade away.
Brother, friend, companion,
come alive.
"Now is the time,"
I hear the great mystery say.

It's time to catch up with Jesus,
welcome rivulets of wonder.
It's time to celebrate
unbidden bursts of love
washing upon creation.

This Clay Jar

In this clay jar,
the dust from which I came,
fragile, ancient and new.

I pray with anxiety in my soul,
may this virus-ridden world
carry forth the wisdom of the Earth.

May we build sandcastles
on the shore of life,
as we shape, polish and pray.

May we bring to this mysterious moment
the call of the Great Spirit,
who promises an adventurous plunge
into what this clay can be.

The Call of Integral Ecology

In his groundbreaking work *Laudato Si'*, on care for our common home, Pope Francis provided an articulation of integral ecology for the first time in the history of our tradition. He said that "a great cultural, spiritual, and educational challenge stands before us and it will demand that we set out on the long path of renewal." In this prophetic work, the Pope offered a vision that captures the ministry of Springbank Retreat.

For more than thirty years, this sacred site in the pinewood forest has welcomed seekers from around the country and across the world. They have come here for prayer, rest, and the transformation of consciousness.

The Springbank ministry continues to be responsive to the signs of the times. My book *Geo Justice: The Emergence of Integral Ecology* captures the essence of our vision. It is a call to all people of good will to listen and respond to the needs of those who are poor or passed by.

Mainstream culture favors corporations and dismisses the needs of those in poverty who call out for social change. We hear that call from the cottonfields of South Carolina to the doorsteps of the halls of justice around the country. We hear it from those who are overwhelmed by the pandemic and whose health and economic status have been diminished and disregarded by the comfortable and well-off during these early years of the twenty-first century.

Here at Springbank Retreat, we listen with the ear of our hearts as we witness the diminishment of divine presence in our midst. Today's ecological devastation of the Earth offends and desecrates the panentheistic vision held at Springbank. As we turn to the ecological vision of Pope

Francis, we understand the diminishment of the divine presence as the tearing of a page from sacred scripture.

Through the programs we offer at Springbank, we aim to create a turning point in human/Earth history, as we search for a better way ahead. We strive to provide a new vision for a new world, one that we consider an operational vision for our time today.

We are simultaneously aware of the failed presidency of Donald Trump and of the healing words of Pope Francis, who invites us to dream. We acknowledge the prophetic visions of Leonardo Boff and Thomas Berry, whose scholarship and vision provided the foundation for *Laudato Si'*.

Dreams and Visions

I have a dream today
that our climate will be restored,
poverty will cease,
the children will be cherished,
everyone will have a home,
beauty will shine forth,
justice will be met,
peace will surround us,
the unimaginable will happen.

Yes, all things will change.
The world will be amazing.
Nothing is impossible.
Blessed be change.
Thank you for transformation.
Let hope rise among us.
Amen.

Jim Conlon

Combustion

Impulse, angst, desire
and fear of outburst
hover in the recesses
of my heart.
At this crossroads of my life,
I pray that forgiveness
will be possible,
that the past can be left behind.
For it is not possible
to sleepwalk into tomorrow.

Jim Conlon

Prayer for Integral Ecology

Mother Earth, I hear your cry.
Brother River, I feel your thirst.
May the great spirit flow within your heart,
bring peace to an anxious world.

Creator God, source of wisdom,
may we listen with our hearts
to the cry of Earth, whose sacred body
is source of beauty, life and food.

Be with us now, as we anticipate the days ahead.
Join us as all God's children
await the day when divine creative energy
will bring hope and wonder to our cosmic home.

Privilege and Power

What a ragged tale we weave,
privilege and power
are our clear and present danger.
Whatever happened
to integrity and truth?

Is this not our time,
when love shall pour forth
like a mighty stream,
quench our parched land,
invigorate our anxious spirit?

May each grace-filled moment
bring truth and empowerment to all.
Amen.

To Be Transparent

Often we hear people speak about the need to be transparent. I think it is really about honesty, about telling the truth.

We are challenged in life to heal the divisions and differences that divide us. We must heal any acts of deception through our honesty and truthfulness.

Thomas Merton encouraged us to see and practice this in our lives. He called on us to be our true self, and to avoid covering and camouflaging that true, transparent self.

Throughout our lives, we may cover over who we really are. Harm can occur when we lack discipline and truth. When we deceive ourselves and speak without accuracy about things we know that are not true, the result is anger, outrage, and the refusal to take responsibility for our actions.

Creating a false self and presenting that false self to the world sets up dualism in the soul. This deceptive patterning has its origins in childhood and in our lack of discipline. It continues as we promote deception in our image. This robs us of an authentic manifestation of who we really are and can become.

Here at Last

I am here at last.
Yes, dear ones,
I am here at last.

I sink slowly
into the silent forest,
listen to the birds' a cappella song
welcome the sun.

I say yes to the rain,
see the four-leggeds
frolic in the meadow,
dance among the trees.

May each new creation
tell Earth what it is meant to be.
Embrace ripples of beauty
all around—yes, all around!

Jim Conlon

Echoes

Bluster and noise,
bluster and noise,
echo repeatedly
in the chamber of my heart.

Now is the time, dear friends,
to announce to all present,
"May those who missed the mark
not be forgotten this day."

Listen deeply
with the ear of the heart.
Stand up for justice,
peace and Earth.

Dismiss the bluster and noise.
Create a new echo
in the chamber of your heart.
Act now, my friends, act now.

God's Dream

Through the years, dreams have been an important way for people to gain access to the adventures of society and soul. Thomas Berry reminded us that Earth and all of creation are manifestations of God's dream. He also said that our participation in the evolutionary process of Earth is in fact our great work.

The pain and pathology of this moment have arisen because our dreams of progress have crashed. What is required from us today is human participation in the awesome liturgy of the universe. Our challenge is to go back to our genetic imperative and reinvent our culture. To accomplish this, we need a new revelatory vision and a transformed consciousness.

Jim Conlon

Just Pray

Holy mystery,
breath of all,
be with us now.
Just pray.

Be with all that is.
Pray with your life.
Depend on it.
Feel the heart beat.

Experience God.
Awaken,
feel this present moment.
There is nothing else to do,
just pray.

You are on your way to God.
Fall in love with life.
Just pray.
Yes, just pray.

Dynamic Integration

Teilhard de Chardin spoke of a new human experience and possibility. His theology healed the dualism between the historical Jesus and the Cosmic Christ. Suddenly the beyondness of God became an operative way of viewing the world. His dynamic integration healed the great dualism between God and Earth.

We now understand that our relationship to the divine and to the Earth happens through an integrated approach. With this dynamic integration of God and Earth, we become empowered and capable of serving in and through the Earth. In this evolutionary way, we heal even in the midst of darkness and division.

We heal the toxins around us and we experience the healing serum of compassion, which cleanses, purifies, and protects each creature, great and small. We heal what is broken and renew the face of the Earth. It is time for each of us to follow the star of creativity and intuition that guides us into unimaginable places

Today we are reminded of that ancient moment almost fourteen billion years ago when divinity flowed forth out of nothingness and became present as it is today. We step back and listen to the unrest in our country and the world and pray that we may become instruments of harmony, balance, and peace during these pandemic times.

May the virus that has descended upon this country and the world be healed by serums, and friendship restored to the Earth and its people.

Fragile Hope

There is a hope in my heart that wants to live,
an enduring promise for which I struggle and strive.

May each day be filled with hope
as I reach out to friend and foe alike.

See beyond your shattered dreams and dare to hope
 again.
May this fragile moment be filled with promise.

Patience

You don't have to run after it.
It was there all the time.
All you have to do is wait.
Yes, creator God,
it was there all the time.
Patience is everything.

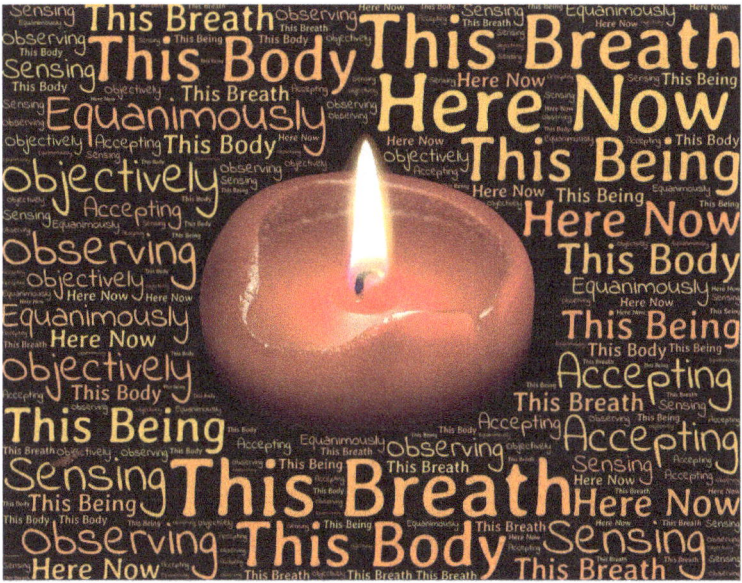

The Tunnel and the Green Door

Throughout history, humanity has searched with fresh urgency for meaning in our lives, for answers to our deepest questions. Through cycles of struggle as well as fulfillment, we rise and fall, again and again. In each sacred moment, we die to ourselves and rise to a concern for people and the planet. Each day, our lives emerge into a new radiant moment in human/Earth history.

As planetary people, our lives are guided by an updraft of awareness that propels us into engagement, in a world whose transformation has yet to be experienced. As people of symbolic consciousness, we venture forth empowered by the metaphor of "the tunnel and the green door."

The tunnel represents the challenges we face, having been born into an unfinished universe. Here we take up the challenge to make our contribution to the world by moving the evolutionary universe forward. We respond to the sacred impulse that invites us to bring more beauty to our world.

The tunnels of our lives are its obstacles and blocked passages. They also represent an opportunity for liberation and fulfillment, a time for prophetic acts that free us from oppression and whatever holds us back from becoming the people we are destined to be. Tunnels are reminders of what we may confront each day: the passing of a loved one, the dissolving of a friendship, the loss of a dream, defeat on the ball field or rink, an unexpected diagnosis, and unforeseen surprises that upset our plans.

Yet despite the tunnels in our lives, we still experience the call to take our place and accomplish whatever needs to be done to bring beauty, peace, and wonder to our endangered planet. The green door represents that opportunity for upliftment.

As we "fall upward" into life, we ponder the question posed by Mary Oliver: "Tell me, what do you plan to do with your one wild and precious life?" Questions like this are asked daily in every person's life—by parents, millennials, political leaders, religious leaders, and others of influence. To respond adequately requires a profound sensitivity to the movement of the holy spirit, an interior awareness that could be seen as the GPS of the soul.

Enhancing our sensitivity to the promptings, the impulses, of the true Self, we become open and transparent, vulnerable and sensitive, to the joys and sorrows of this time. We can then eagerly respond to the call of the people and the planet. This indeed is the green door through which we must all walk.

Broken Mirror

Ask yourself,
What do I see
in this broken mirror?

Perhaps it's the day
you fell and scraped your knee
on the fractured sidewalk
in front of your house.
Or the day you failed
a class in high school,
watched your future shatter.

Perhaps your days
became broken mirrors,
each reflecting back
your hopes and dreams,
shining fragments of your
as-yet-unlived life.

Jim Conlon

Pay Attention

Pay attention to the flowers.
Pay attention to the bees.
Watch how they pray.
Watch your soul.
Notice the cosmos.
Notice water and trees.
Pay attention, my friend.
Fall upon your knees.
Let your body pray.
Yes, pay attention dear friend.
Let your body pray.
Now.

Is there anything
more precious,
more immediate,
on our way to prayer
than each undefended moment
that wraps my trembling soul
in the amazing mystery
of this sacred now?

Jim Conlon

Transgenetic Cultural Coding

We as humans contribute to the ongoing work of creation through a process Thomas Berry called *transgenetic cultural coding*.

To understand this, first we have to understand the distinction between genetic coding and transgenetic cultural coding.

Most creatures do not possess self-reflective consciousness. How they act and react is determined by their very nature—their genetic coding. For example, an ant is genetically coded to build an anthill. There is little variance within their insect culture. The differences that do exist are determined by their specific ant species. However, no ant will be guided by the coding of a beaver or a frog. Only beavers are genetically coded to build dams.

Because humans have the gift of self-reflection, we are able to imagine and create a variety of responses to the need for building a community. The result might be a condominium, a high-rise apartment, a cottage in the suburbs, or something else. Similarly, music is an expression of culture and environment. All of this is possible because of transgenetic cultural coding. This ability to harness human memory, imagination, and experience makes it possible for us to create what was previously unimagined. It makes it possible for us to go beyond mere genetic coding. It makes it possible for us to fashion a second birth for ourselves and all of humanity.

When we become people of the new cosmology and the new story, we have the capacity to create a synthesis between the human and the other-than-human worlds. We are able to affirm that all of creation is sacred. We realize that the universe is a communion, and everything is connected with everything else. In fact, everything is a continuous reality and each of us is able to see that we are members of a bioregional Earth community.

Jim Conlon

A Second Birth

Wrestling with the prophets
is indeed our call.
Reimagining wisdom
is our life.
Imagining a second birth
is our challenge.

Listen to the silence
that you hear.
It's filled with gratitude and hope.
Discover the place
where you belong,
where everything is healed.

Virus Prayer

Hospitality expressed,
discernment revisited,
the quest continues:
What's next for us all?

Illness surrounds us,
tomorrow is unclear.
What is the message
we all want hear?

I pray with my feet,
give thanks for this day.
I hear wisdom say,
"Tomorrow is a mystery."

Listen, pay attention today,
embrace every question.
Don't worry, be present.
Just pray.

Jim Conlon

Message to the World

I believe we are here for a reason,
to bring a message to the world,
to heal the turmoil of these days
with the silence of our hearts.

We are compelled to say to the world,
to all who dare to listen,
bring healing to this abandoned place,
say yes to all who care.

Heal what is broken,
bind up the wounds,
say your prayers,
allow peace to wash upon creation.

Goodbye Joey

Dear Joey, friend of Earth and Springbank,
you taught us many things.
How to wake each morning.
How to live among the trees,
enjoy breakfast with your friends,
snuggle with Trina in the night.

Thomas Merton told us about you,
and he was correct:
"Every four-legged creature is a saint."
Goodbye, dear friend,
as you dance among the trees,
and be at peace, be at peace.

Jim Conlon

Listen and Pray

The world is a poem,
full of beauty, brokenness and soul.
Each day is a song of beauty,
a passage, a page, of all the stories
that I have yet to tell.

Radiant sunshine flows across the land,
bringing radiance,
pasturing hope.
Horizons of expectation
stretch across the vast azure sky.

I hear each heart say,
"May the melodies of wonder
dance across the cosmos,
allowing each new moment
to gather, listen and pray."

Silence

We the people
must drastically change.
On this anniversary
of Earth Day,
we are immersed in virus,
hovering at the edge,
calling for the courage
of the heart.

I mourn the death
of so many souls,
now silent.
May there be a rising
not yet known,
a sacred time
when beauty
will restore the world.

Jim Conlon

Icon of Glory

Glory and praise!
We recall, remember and proclaim
the transfigured Christ,
shining forth
with an incandescent glow.

Alive, vital and transformed,
a beacon for this time,
shine brilliantly
into an ever-awakening dawn.
Every image is a scriptural verse.

People of the Planet

As people of this planet, we are called to embrace in an intimate way the experience of continuous searching.

We encounter both the joys and sorrows of our time through this continuous and open-ended journey.

We ponder and discern the sacred impulses that prompt us to penetrate into the depths of what lies ahead.

Guided by spirit, we allow ourselves to see all that is before us in an undefended and transparent way.

We never forget the poor and neglected as we follow the wisdom of those closest to the problem, while also increasing our awareness of each awesome moment.

In this way, we internalize the radiant cosmic energy that flows like a river of grace.

The Quest for a Quantum Theology

Science, religion, and culture are all required as we look into the future.

In particular, we are challenged to create a dynamic synthesis between science and religion. Diarmuid O'Murchu describes the cutting-edge intersection of physics and spirituality as *quantum theology*.

Empirical science guides us with facts that can be measured and used to create our future. As we anticipate what is to come, we also seek the guidance of our inherited wisdom tradition. Broadly speaking, this tradition encompasses the various world religions, such as Christianity, Judaism, and Islam.

We are challenged to develop a new cultural wisdom that is born out of both the resources of our souls and our empirical observations. Some might call this as a second birth, or a *cultural rebirth*.

We cannot realize our fullest potential if we are only guided by our existing cultural conditioning. We need a cultural rebirth to move forward in a way that synthesizes science and religion. It will also involve a synthesis of bioregional and cultural experience.

This kind of guidance is not available to us from our religious tradition. To achieve a proper vision and practice requires a synthesis of panentheistic theology and contemporary cultural moments so we can respond to the reality before us.

Almost Persuaded

Remember the joy of tomorrow,
plan memories now past.
Today we ponder what's next,
give thanks as chapters unfold.

Every day bought unexpected heartaches,
sometimes unexpected peace.
I ponder this day, then wonder
what this turning point means.

Today you dream of tomorrow,
wonder what's up ahead.
Look within, then yonder,
on this almost persuaded new day.

Jim Conlon

Goodbye

TV turned off,
door almost locked,
no one at dinner
to bid me goodbye.

I look down the side road,
try not to cry,
say hello to emptiness
as nobody waves goodbye.

I gather my memories
of good times and sad,
embrace that emptiness
as I go without goodbye.

My Justice Work

Throughout the years I have struggled to discover how best to present myself to the world. Early in life, my mind was clouded with uncertainty and doubt; however, I was deeply energized following the Vatican II Council.

Looking back now, I can see that I was in a privileged position but I lacked discipline. You could say that I was spoiled.

On one occasion, I responded to the invitation of a parishioner of the Sacred Heart Church in London asking if I would be interested in supporting a program to house single displaced persons in the city. The man who invited me was a recovering alcoholic and sensitive to the needs of the homeless and displaced.

I befriended a minister who had dedicated his life to feeding the hungry and housing the homeless in downtown London. This was my first participation in a justice project during my parish ministry work. I also visited classes at St. Patrick High School in London.

My first two years following ordination were with Fr. Zimmney. He was a former faculty member of the seminary and a well-respected priest in the diocese.

One day the phone rang. It was Greg Blonde, who was the bishop's secretary. The call was a message from Bishop Gerald Emmett Carter, inviting me to meet him. When we met, he announced that my next assignment would be in Stratford with Fr. O'Rourke. He had a reputation in the diocese for being tough on young priests.

When I heard this news from the bishop, I swallowed hard and accepted the assignment.

During the following days, I was overwhelmed with anxiety and unable to sleep. I was generally worried about my future.

I shared my upset with my pastor, Fr. Zimmney. As a former faculty member, he knew Monsignor Laverty, who had been the bursar of the seminary and was now the vicar general of the diocese.

Because my anxiety was increasing, Fr. Zimmney asked if I would speak with Msgr. Laverty. With a sigh of relief, I responded in the affirmative.

Not many days later, I was again summoned to speak to the bishop. When I arrived, I learned that my assignment had been changed. I was to report to Fr. Gerry Frecker at Our Lady of Mercy Church in Sarnia.

I drove my 1956 Chevrolet, a gift of my Uncle John, to my next post in Sarnia. It was an important transition in my pastoral work.

Dawn

It's morning,
dawn in the forest,
silent here among the trees.
Discover how to listen
to the breeze.
Here I walk and wonder.
Here I make my plea.
May tomorrow
bring us wisdom,
reveal the lyrics of a song.

JIM CONLON

Thank you, John Lewis

John Lewis, peacemaker, troublemaker,
friend of freedom seekers,
your life, your courage, your nonviolent action
inspire us and call us forth today.

Your vision of justice on the bridge in Selma
and on so many bridges you called us to cross
is deep in each soul—
bridges for black and white,
bridges for equal pay,
bridges for a safe place to live and raise children,
bridges of "I shall not be moved,"
bridges of perseverance and forgiveness,
bridges that make us all one.

Silently Waiting

We sit here silently today.
This is a day of waiting:
waiting for time to pass,
waiting for friends to call,
waiting and wondering,
what tomorrow will bring.

Wondering today why our planet is sick,
waiting for tomorrow for friendship,
waiting for air to breathe,
waiting for a world that is just,
waiting for a time
when all can be free.

Jim Conlon

From Fragility to Truth

It is so easy to deny one is racist,
so easy at times to deny what is true.
In this pain-filled world,
denial can be a subtle thing,
a shelter from growth, from love.
Today is my memory day.
It is so hard to admit fragility,
so hard to see it is what we need now
to unlock true memory,
to become again what we were
in the beginning,
all one.

My New Assignment

My new assignment was a doorway into one of the most meaningful years of my pastoral ministry.

Pastor Gerry Frecker was open and engaged and responsive to the needs of people. Msgr. Lowrey, who had been a priest for many years, lived in residence. He was a patriarchal figure for the people; however, he did not interfere with the things of the parish and primarily kept to himself.

During my Sarnia years, I was fortunate to become involved in several projects. There was a building in Sarnia that had been designated to be torn down. Meanwhile, it was available for occupancy.

In cooperation with four neighboring congregations—Anglican, Presbyterian, United Church of Christ, and Our Lady of Mercy Church—we developed what we called the 404 House. We provided breakfast and dinner for homeless men and on occasion gave them referrals for possible employment. The program was financed by the four congregations, each of which offered $100 a month. A man was hired to live in the building and supervise the occupants.

Another initiative we called the Downtown House. It was situated on Front Street in Sarnia. This project was cosponsored by the four downtown churches and was coordinated by volunteers from the various congregations. Community people could come during the day to play cards and share in conversation. In the evening, it served as a gathering place for young people so they could be off the street and safe.

One day, a young man whose father was the director of a nearby funeral home knocked at the door. He asked if I would be willing to have my name proposed as a candidate for the young man of the year. I was honored and surprised. In the end, another candidate, who was well known for his participation as an Olympic athlete, was selected, and rightfully so; however, it was an honor to have my name proposed.

There were many young adults in Our Lady of Mercy Church and in the wider community. I cooperated with their leaders to form a social program to support their needs and to provide companionship for them. On occasion, we raised money for needy causes. We called the group Sarnia's Swinging Singles, a name well suited for a group whose participants were generous and engaged in the community.

I participated in exhibition hockey. The participants were called Saints and Sinners—saints referred to the clergy, and sinners to members of the press.

After my time at Our Lady of Mercy Church, I went to St. Agnes in Chatham. I looked forward to working with my new pastor, Fr. Charlie Sylvester.

I was supervised by a new pastor, Fr. Jack Boyde, who opted to become a travel agent and later married. It was only after I moved to St. Ursula's that I heard about the accusations that were made about him. As a result, he was sent to the penitentiary for pedophilia. As he left the courtroom, on his way to prison, he asked for forgiveness. I wrote to him and addressed the letter to his sister. Subsequently, I received the unwelcome news of his death in prison, which startled me and caused unrest that lingered for months.

Jim Conlon

How Can This Be?

I feel alone today,
disconnected and afraid,
all by myself
in this wondrous world.
How can this be?

Today amidst sunshine
and a fresh warming breeze,
alone among the trees,
I breathe a soft prayer:
how can this be?

I watch the television,
as healers and companions
wait for good news,
I listen, breathe and pray:
how can this be?

Today the clouds lift,
yes, beauty returns,
as I once again ask,
tell me, please tell,
how can this be?

Jim Conlon

Questions

What do I respond
when my world falls to pieces,
when all seems tattered and torn?

To whom do I turn
when my direction seems lost,
when a blurred future appears?

Then I step back and breathe,
allow balance to return,
chart a way forward.
Find freedom today.

Portals of the Heart

May all fragmentation cease.
Discover God in the little things
you do extraordinarily well.

Open the portals of your heart.
See within, this mystery—
God is everywhere.

O shaper of the future,
may your imagination thrive.
The future is yours to create.

In Toronto and Chicago

One day, Fr. Sylvester and I attended a program conducted by Dr. Ed File in Windsor. Ed was the founder of the Canadian Urban Training Project for Christian Service (CUT) in Toronto. He was a United Church minister, held a doctorate in urban sociology, and was on the faculty of York University. Following his presentation that afternoon, I applied to be a candidate for a program in Toronto.

I received a rather ambiguous approval from the bishop and Fr. Sylvester. Following my journey to Toronto to join the CUT program, I took up residence at St. Augustine's Seminary in Scarboro. My time at the CUT program involved a year-long placement on the staff of the Riverdale Community Organization (RCO). They had an office on Gerard St., just east of the Dawn Valley Parkway. My supervisor was Don Keating, a United Church minister from Winnipeg, Manitoba, who had participated in programs on community organization in Chicago.

My RCO year was very strenuous and challenging. Although I felt lonely and isolated, something in me compelled me to soldier on.

My brother spoke to me one day at Aunt Margaret's home concerning my move to Toronto. He asked if I was on my way to leaving the priesthood. I challenged his suggestion, although deep inside I felt uncertain about the future.

I am grateful to Don Keating for suggesting that I call Msgr. Jack Egan, whose organization was the Catholic Committee on Urban Ministry (CCUM). My time at CUT was coming to a close when Msgr. Egan responded to my call and suggested that I visit him at Notre Dame

University, where he was recovering from a severe heart attack.

I found my way to Notre Dame, and to Jack's office. I told him my story and said I didn't know what was next in my life. Jack listened. As I sat in his office, the phone continued to ring. The callers were a cross section of people who were leading significant programs across the country. Among them were Geno Baroni, Phil Murnion, Marjorie Tuite, Saul Alinsky, Ed Chambers, and Richard Harmon.

Finally Jack said, "I'll write to your bishop, whom I remember meeting in Rome at the Vatican Council, and tell him I'll keep an eye on you. And I'll ask whether you can come to Chicago. I'm on the board of Urban Training Center for Christian Mission and the Industrial Area Foundation Saul Alinsky Training Institute, and I can arrange for you to attend these programs. The experience will prepare you for the future."

Following the visit to Notre Dame University, I returned to complete my program in Toronto. And, as suggested by Jack, I made an appointment with Bishop Carter in London.

When I entered his office, the letter from Jack was on his desk. As our conversation ended, I was granted permission to study in Chicago and to enroll in two programs where Jack was on the board of directors.

Those of us working in the urban training program were housed in the local YMCA. The train that passed by my window made sleep difficult. However, those days marked a turning point in my life. Without the support and intervention of Msgr. Egan, my life today would be quite different.

The Midway Organization (TMO) became my base of operation. I met frequently with Richard Harmon to plan the next steps in the TMO adventure.

Following the culmination of the TMO program, it became clear that my time in Chicago had ended. Jack invited me to attend the annual gathering of CCUM. At that time, I had no plans for the future and did not foresee a role in the church.

It was time to return to Canada. Because London was a rural diocese, Jack suggested I would be better off in Toronto, having been trained for urban work.

When I returned to Toronto, I spent a few days with my friend Peter, who was living in a house group on Brunswick Avenue. Then I moved into a room at St. Michael's College. I was able to secure a $5000 grant from a local initiative project of the federal government and provided an office in Toronto's West End YMCA. There I founded the West Central project and began to work in community organization.

I was fortunate to meet Vince Battistelli, who worked at Humber. We wrote a proposal that we called the Institute for Communities in Canada. We published a small magazine called *Interaction*. The advisory council members included Gregory Baum and Mary Jo Leddy.

I continued my organizational work at Humber and focused on the low-income community of the Jane-Finch area. I also taught a course on community organization and development for students who were preparing to work in the local area.

During my years at Humber, there was a rule in place that allowed me to function without collecting payment from the participants. However, that situation did not last. One day, Ken Meckerrger spoke to me about the financial changes at the college. He said I was welcome to continue teaching at Humber but I would have to generate funds by selling courses in the community. As a result, I began to reconsider my time in Humber and look for an alternative means of employment.

I applied for a position with the Canadian Mental Health Association (CMHA) in downtown Toronto. The director of the program was Audrey McLaughlin, a well-known member of the New Democratic Party (NDP), who came from Canada's Northwest Territory. When asked if I would have a problem working with a woman, I indicated that I would not.

During this time, the federal government was offering locally initiated project grants. The process allowed for programs to receive money to sponsor local programs. Together we designed a program called Friends and Advocates. Sylvia Moustakis was hired to direct the program. The goal of the program was to provide information and support for people being discharge from mental hospitals. It was quite successful, and we were able to secure permanent funding from the province of Ontario.

Shortly after, I applied to teach a course in pastoral theology called Emerging Forms of Ministry at Toronto School of Theology (TST). The class focused on supporting participants as they designed programs for whatever needed to be done. The class was well received, and participants designed programs on such topics as support for those who are developmentally challenged.

One day while still working at CMHA, Remi Le Mouges informed me that he would be leaving his post soon because the Jesuit community had asked him to take over the management of the Ignation community in Guelph, Ontario. I applied for and was offered his position as assistant director of TST, with responsibility for the field of education and pastoral training.

When I received the call from the director of TST, Dr. Doug Jay, he asked if I was involved with Therafields, a hypnotherapy program developed by Lea Hindley-Smith that was popular at the time. I said I knew some people but had no direct contact with it.

This was a significant turning point in my relationship with the church. It was a position that I previously not thought possible. I was able to apply my experience in urban training in community organization to my new responsibilities at TST.

Jim Conlon

An Uncertain Pilgrim

It seems forever
since I wondered about the future and the call.
So many days have passed since then,
yes, so many days.

Yet today I feel called to write,
to tell you about my pain,
the fear that hovers in my awareness.
Despite it all, I hear the call.

It is a call that invites me to life,
to what at one time seemed intolerable
and unimaginable,
yet still calls me forth today.

Awash in the virus and uncertain votes,
I dare to dream again of days
of beauty and of peace.
May we uncertain pilgrims
be ready for the days ahead.

New Year's Day

What time is it in the Universe?

We live in a time, a developmental time.
No longer confined to linear time,
our future evolves, day after day,
as we step aside
from a world no longer static and stuck.

The grandfather clock,
resting stately on the wall
no longer determines where we are.
Now is the time to wonder,
what time is it in the Universe?

At the Toronto School of Theology

During my years at TST, we began the program Catholics for Social Change. It was a facilitator of the Labor Day Statements of the Canadian Bishops for local and national gatherings. Among these were a Society to be Transformed and From Words to Action. Eventually we expanded the outreach of Catholics for Social Change into an annual event, and we named the program Institute in Christian Life in Canada. Even today I receive the proceedings of those events.

I focused primarily on community organization and social justice. I had not read beyond social justice in the context of community organization, yet I sensed a growing interest in spirituality. We formed a committee at TST to explore the impact of spirituality on the practice of ministry. I met an Anglican priest named Ron Fellows who was the director of the Applewood Center for Spirituality, and he became a member of our TST committee.

Ron invited me to attend a summer program on spirituality that took place at York University. The headliner of the program was Matthew Fox, a Dominican priest from the Midwest who had created a program at Mundelein College in Chicago. At the time, he was in a conversation with the administration of Holy Names University. The plan was to move his program from Chicago to Oakland in 1983. The name of the program was the Institute in Creation Centered Spirituality (ICCS).

I arrived late for the program that was being held in York University in Toronto. When I entered the large gymnasium-like room, a man, slim in stature, with a shock of white hair, was leading a circle dance. The man was

Matthew Fox, the leader of the program to be held that summer.

As the days passed, I had the opportunity to meet Matthew and have a conversation. Ron Fellows arranged for us to have lunch. During the week, we walked down Younge Street to support the United Farm Workers' lettuce boycott. On another occasion, I share with Matthew that I was coming up for a sabbatical leave the following year and had no plans for it yet.

Later that summer, I flew out to California for a few days. There I met Alexandra Kovats and Brian Swimme, who were on the staff of the program. After returning to Toronto, I applied to take my sabbatical leave in Oakland the following fall. Later that summer, Matthew and Brian came to conduct a program in Toronto. His book *Original Blessing* was released on that weekend.

Years earlier, I had attended a conference in London at the Ontario Hospital, a government facility for psychiatric patients. There, a friend introduced me to Gregory Baum, one of Canada's best-known theologians and a Peritti (that is to say, a theological expert of Vatican Council II). At one point when Gregory was visiting London, he introduced me to a man named Peter whose sister, Mary Lou, was involved in Therafields. Because of my friendship with Peter and Mary Lou, I drove to Toronto to enter communications therapy. Peter was already involved, and a friend named Joe Leonard was also interested. We began to have weekly sessions in Toronto and called ourselves the "road team." This began a weekly routine of driving to Toronto for personal sessions as well as meeting together in a group.

Eventually we were invited to participate in a Catholic group that was a collection of thirty to forty people, many of whom were religious sisters and priests. The group became somewhat notorious in Toronto. The archbishop of Toronto, Philip Pocock, was upset about the program because the participants would leave their vocations and pursue an alternative way of life. This was true for both Peter and Joe. Each of them left and married. Although I was uncertain, I was not free enough nor did I want to follow their example. I valued my ties with the Catholic Church, and for some time, I vacillated about my future role in the church

Following my urban training in Toronto as well as urban training and community organization in Chicago, I was fortunate to remain in good standing with the church. I felt guided by a providential grace during those years of ambiguity and uncertainty. Today I can say with Patrick Kavanaugh how proud I am to have claimed my inheritance. I made good friends and learned about the struggle and now can give thanks for all that made it possible for me to be where I am today.

Uncertainty

Today our world
totters on uncertainty.
We must dare to ask
if in its far-off fragile days,
the future shall be filled
with glory or demise.

I breathe in a moment
of peace and cosmic hope.
May all poison
immersed in air, water, and land
be healed, purified and cease.

Take up the challenge now.
Flow into all,
keep going, with fresh promise.
Despite the uncertain face
of evidence,
all is not lost.

JIM CONLON

Forgiveness

What does it mean
to look back and pray
for forgiveness?
When at times we failed,
did it not happen
when we were rescued
and survived unexpectedly,
to live again?
Today I ask,
how am I to paint
the landscape of my soul
and inscribe the pattern
of love and letting go?

Moving Westward

In the early 1980s, the church in Toronto was undergoing deep changes, and a cloud of suspicion hung over it. In many ways, it was a good time to leave and an appropriate turning point for me to be open to new learning and challenges.

One could say that Cardinal Carter was cleaning house at St. Augustine's seminary. He replaced the director, and one of the best-known faculty members took a position in Edmonton, Alberta.

Meanwhile, the Therafields experiment was beginning to calcify and shows signs of decay. Lea Hindley-Smith was suffering from diabetes, and her influence on the Therafields community was in deep decline. I began to feel it was a good time to leave.

Around the same time, a friend in Toronto suggested I would do well to go to Esalen in California to explore a work-scholar program. I had heard about Dr. Stan Grof and decided to enroll in his program.

My time in Esalen was fruitful and I learned a great deal from Stan and Christina Grof. Dr. Grof had recently published a book about his work, titled *Beyond the Brain*. I welcomed the opportunity to study at Esalen and to learn the practice of holotropic breath work.

When my work-study project at Esalen was complete, it was time to move on to Holy Names University.

Jim Conlon

Only God Could Know

God of the Cosmos,
source of love and life,
sprinkle your presence
generously across the azure sky.
Each new sacred moment
brings trimmings of wonder
to decorate the awesome vista.
Dance across the depths
and peer into unexpected places
that only God could know—
yes, crevices and depths
that only God could know.

A Song in My Heart

There is a song in my heart
that wants to sing,
a wound in my soul
that wants to heal.

May this be a time
to influence the trajectory of life,
be guided by the stars
and find meaning in the path ahead.

Forecast

I see wisdom up ahead.
So bid the past goodbye.
Shatter yesterday in your heart.
Gaze into the new year and
prepare for what is yet to come.

At Holy Names University

When I came to Holy Names University in California in 1984, I came for a one-semester sabbatical leave. At that time, I had no capacity to work in the United States nor a future before me; however, something propelled me to go forward.

In the final days of August 1984, I traveled back to the Bay Area. On the first of many mornings, I went to the Fruitvale BART station and took bus #54 to the Holy Names University campus. Moments later, I walked into a meeting room and saw seated around the table the staff members of the graduate program at ICCS. In the room were both Matthew Fox, the founder and director of the program, and Brian Swimme, whose book *The Universe is a Green Dragon* was about to be published in a few weeks. Also present was Alexandra Kovats, well-known spiritual director and co-program director with Brian. She had just published her masters' project, *Prayer: A Discovery of Life*. Also present was Brendan Doyle, a musician and admissions councilor. All of these people had come from Mundelien College in Chicago. They were the ICCS staff preparing for the fall semester.

Even though I was included in the staff meeting, my background had not prepared me for the days ahead. My background was in communication therapy, urban training, and community organization. I had little preparation or experience in culture and spirituality and had not studied or read the work of Brain and Matthew. However, I was assigned to facilitate a process seminar group.

During my first year, I lived in Hildegard House with the students. It was a former convent. My responsibility was to collect the rent and participate on the faculty as well.

Eventually I was able to attain immigration status so I could work legally and earn a salary at the university.

Later I was assigned to teach the overview class on each Monday morning. The text was always the *Original Blessing*. I found the focus of creation-centered spirituality attractive because it was organized into four paths, culminating in a via transformativa justice.

My journey became one of healing the dualism between science and religion, and ultimately to create a dynamic integration between science, society and religion. I began to see the universe as the developing reality engaged in a series of irreversible moments that began with the great flaring forth fourteen billion years ago and evolved into galaxies, solar systems, planet, life, and eventually humans.

This understanding give birth to an evolutionary story of the universe as a process replete with energy. I began to feel the stars above and below me. This vision gave birth to a profound sense of wonder that was thrilling, hopeful, and unfinished.

One evening when Brian was teaching, I came to the realization that the new cosmology was a source of great wisdom that each human with self-reflective consciousness has the capacity to be fully human. We are, as Brian would say, at the cusp of being born again into a culture of creativity. We need to understand the new cosmology so we can receive guidance for the days ahead.

Sophia Center

Throughout my life, I have had an enduring desire to create a program, a project, a book that would be remembered and considered significant. Following thirteen years of working with Matthew Fox at Holy Names, we inaugurated the Sophia Center, a wisdom school celebrating Earth, art, and spirit.

Those were treacherous times in the church, especially with regard to the writings of progressive theologians. We heard echoes of these challenges from Cardinal Ratzinger, who later became the Pope. On one occasion, Matthew took out a one-page ad in the *New York Times*, which he addressed to Ratzinger and the people of the world. He accused Ratzinger of being the leader of a dysfunctional church.

When Matthew approached me to take sides with him against the university, I responded that I did not have the authority to act as he wished and that the request needed to be referred to the university administration. The result of this standoff was his dismissal from the Dominican community. Matthew continued at Holy Names University but began to function as an Episcopal priest. He was guided in this process by a former Roman Catholic priest who had himself become an Episcopal priest. With a sense of humor, he said he did not want to lose his ecclesiastical driver's license, so he would continue to function as a priest. For some time, he promoted the Techno Cosmic Mass, which he had adopted from the work of Chris Brain, the leader of the community in England. Later, he was welcomed into the Episcopal Church.

Following Matthew's departure, I was asked by the administration to continue the program in spirituality. I met with the remaining faculty to find a new name for the program. The administration provided $10,000 to launch this new effort. The name that was first recommended was Scola Sofia. However, the board of directors asked us to change it to Sophia Center. We continued to develop the program, and at one point, announced that the Sophia Center was a wisdom school celebrating Earth, art, and spirit. In the beginning, our enrollment was meager; we had only about seventeen students in the first year. We were in danger of having the program closed for financial reasons.

One day at a Call to Action Conference, I met someone who was looking at our brochures and was interested but unable to enroll because of her work schedule. Based on that conversation, we initiated a weekend program. This made it possible for people to teach who had name recognition but to whom we could not afford to offer a full salary. The result was that Sophia Center was more attractive to potential students. We combined the previous semester format with the new weekend option. We also continued the practice of conducting a summer institute.

After that, the program began to flourish. Brian Swimme was the regular keynote speaker for the summer programs. In the late 1980s and early 2000s, Sophia Center flourished. We had talented students, qualified faculty, and students from various countries beyond the United States. I was invited to present programs in a variety of cities in Canada and United States as well as New Zealand and Ireland. During my time at Holy Names and shortly after, I was able to publish fourteen books. Among the publishers I worked with were Novalis Canada, Twenty-Third Publications, and Wyndham Hall.

Despite these many successes, it became financially difficult to continue the program. When I retired, the number of students was decreasing.

Today as I look back on those years in California, I stop for a moment at the medicine wheel in the live oak forest at Springbank. As I reflect on the intervals of time marked by the cosmic walk, I am joined by Shelly the dog. Deep inside, I feel my walk is a search for meaning—before in California and now here. The search for meaning is in fact a defining question in my life.

Even though I am elderly, I have a perception of the future as open-ended and promising. I feel grateful for the journey and for the many things yet to be accomplished in my life. The way I feel these days is that I want to leave something behind—an idea, a book, a project, a memory. This impulse and longing for immortality reveals the quest for resurrection. In fact, I believe what I long for is eternal life. I trust the sacred impulse and my desire to create something that endures beyond the grave.

Jim Conlon

A Dog's Life

Shelly stretches,
then reclines on the couch,
drifting it seems into a welcoming sleep.
As she sleeps with carefree solitude
in the hermitage,
unaware of the impeachment trial about to begin
and of the virus taking so many lives,
Shelly reminds me of what's important.
There is beauty all around.

Goodbye Teddy

Teddy left us today, September 28.
His journey at Springbank entered a new
    dimension.
In his early years, he was a companion of Ursula.
He frolicked and played in Haddon House.

When Ursula entered eternal life,
Teddy moved on to be with Trina.
He became her cherished friend.
He visited the art room when she
Taught indigenous wisdom and clay.
Often he would rest on the chapel floor
when Trina played the baby grand piano.

Teddy was Trina's spiritual director.
He was her wisdom guide.
He prayed joyfully when she was glad,
was a source of comfort when she was sad.

Goodbye Teddy!
Joey and others of your family welcome you home.

Tomorrow

My mind grows weak, my body tired.
Memories of days long past remain.
Outrage and anger rule the day.
I recall and rest in my home.
I regret that I have not yet made my mark,
I have not accomplished what I hoped to do.
Please prepare the food that we all may eat,
knowing that tomorrow we will rest.

A New Era

What does it mean to recall painful moments from the past, to allow and embrace the lacerations of the soul that have shaken this nation?

A series of irreversible events marks our time on Earth and records the joys and sorrows of each day. In every precious life, there are memorable moments, times of triumph and loss. In each precious and precarious instant, memories hover like a cloud of unknowing.

Yet, continually, life bursts forth into amazing new moments of love and letting go. Each day is a banquet of beauty as well as of brokenness and pain. We remember the crests and valleys of our journey.

At this time of uncertainty and surprise, we dare to peer into the future that is unfolding for the soul of the country and the spirit of its people. We ponder with cautious anticipation the revelation of the as-yet-hidden wisdom that makes itself known each day.

Today the mind and heart of the people have dispelled a winter of darkness. The heart of America has broken open with an outpouring of fresh hope.

Spirits have been lifted. Politicians of all stripes have announced a new cosmic journey.

We gratefully beseech the God of the universe and of all life to unite us and heal the fractures of the nation and invigorate a new era for all.

After the Tumult

After the tumult,
in the wake of the storm,
we stand up for freedom.
May all things be new.

The rapture of gratitude and new life
is replete with an avalanche of beauty.
The stars twinkle in the cosmos,
and mystery is revealed.

Each new moment is
a precious gift as
we tremble in awesome wonder
at the unimaginable sorrow
that is the companionship of joy.

Jim Conlon

Holy Mystery

As I rise from a restful sleep,
I feel deep within
a silent urge that relentlessly
calls out from a vast abyss.

It says to me,
"The time is short,
feel the silence of this day.
Peer into the solitude."

It reminds me,
"Be not afraid,
don't move the way
fear wants you to."

Listen to this call,
to the voice of holy mystery.
It is the wordless wisdom
that speaks the energy of love.

Wrestling with Mystery

Did you ever experience
being caught up
in a dazzling swirl of energy,
erupting from beyond
the pulse of awareness,
living on the edge of what is real?
I glance at the wondrous path ahead.
It is an uncertain place,
where a far-off vision rests.

Jim Conlon

How to Create a Context for Cosmic Fulfillment

To create a new transgenetic context,
we are invited to imagine and make possible
a constellation of energies
that transcend and enhance
what was previously not possible.

To give birth and rewrite previous tendencies,
we awaken to a new time
and the reinvention of society and soul.
We seek a culminating vision
prompted by compassion, creativity and
    transformation.

Tangible and True

There is something in my life
I know I cannot yet explain.
What I mean to say
in this listening moment
is both silence and the voice of God.

Today we wear masks
to prevent the illness
of others and ourselves.
What we feel seems uncertain and unseen,
yet we know it is tangible and true.

The presence and wisdom of the divine
is also hidden silent, joyful and true.
Is it not the ancient One
who speaks to us, comforts us
when we are lonely and afraid?

May this gracious and invisible friend
make the world a place of rest.
May we be always immersed
in the holy mystery that enlightens
and inspires each yearning soul.

Jim Conlon

A Love Letter to the Universe

Throughout history, the believing community has received divine revelation in a variety of ways. Initially, the biblical story of Jesus of Nazareth was communicated through oral tradition, and after a time, the revealed word of God was told in the Bible, including the New Testament and the Hebrew Bible. This story has come down to us through a variety of worldviews. Among them is the worldview of Plato during the time of Augustine. As time passed, the West became infused with the science of Aristotle. Then Thomas Aquinas, a Dominican friar, was invited to Rome. He composed his signature work, the Summa Theologica, there.

The story of Christianity was significantly affected by the Great Plague, also called the Black Death, in the fourteenth century. During that epidemic, many people died. The believing community, who lacked a medical understanding of the disease, was convinced that the loss of so many lives was caused by an angry God. As a result, a fall and redemption approach became common practice among the believing community. Their spirituality was preoccupied with a fear of the divine and with the notion of human fault. Because people were influenced by their memory of the plague and by their fear that something so devastating could occur again, they felt impelled to conquer nature. During this time, the believing community lost its appreciation for the wonder of beauty and belonging to the universe and Earth.

As a new cosmic story rose on the horizon, depravity began to fade and a fresh, new awareness emerged. A new pattern of consciousness unfolded as humanity noticed that new forms of the natural world were appearing from prior forms. This awareness marked the beginning of an evolutionary worldview. A new creation was born. This story, infused with mystery, understood consciousness and soul as being present at the beginning of the universe some 13.8 billion years ago. A remarkable feature of the new story is that the discoveries of empirical observations through science are compatible with the Christian story. In fact, what we learn from science and tradition is amplified and deepened as it is mutually enhanced at this new revelatory moment in human/Earth history. Perhaps the best response to this new moment is that it is a time for celebration.

JIM CONLON

Thomas Tells Our Sacred Story

On a Thursday afternoon in the fall of 1984, Thomas Berry, CP, was the guest at our graduate program on Culture and Spirituality at Holy Names University. Prior to that day, I had frequently heard of Thomas and the annual colloquiums he led at a retreat center on the shores of Lake Erie. Our paths had crossed, but I had not yet met him. His most significant work, *The Dream of the Earth*, would not be published for another four years.

As I listened to his words on that afternoon, I knew the man before me was a person of towering intellect and a special kind of Passionist. He was a member of the Congregation of the Passion, and his passion was enthusiastically expressed in his passion for the Earth. He was seventy years old but he was on the threshold of a new era in his life. Deep in his sensitive soul, he was moved by a foreboding that had enveloped him since childhood and that had overflowed in his heart in an ecstatic moment as he wandered in the meadow across the creek on the property where his family was building a new home. Even early in his life—a time just on the heels of the second industrial revolution—he had sensed the devastation that was about to come. Now he was propelled into the most fruitful years of his great work.

The 1970s and 1980s were a time of existential angst across the Western world. Members of the believing community were unaware of the sacramentality of their tradition. The stories from scripture about the beginning of things seemed distant and incapable of touching the recesses of their souls.

Having read the works of Pierre Teilhard de Chardin, Thomas knew the insights of evolutionary science were compatible with spirit and replete with activating energy. He also saw that the story of the universe as told by science was inadequate in itself because it lacked a sense of the sacred. He was convinced humanity needed a new story to breathe "fresh energy and a zest for life" into the Christian tradition inherited from the Bible.

Thus, the universe story was being born within the mind and heart of Thomas. In the future, he would develop it further, together with evolutionary philosopher Brian Thomas Swimme and scholar of Eastern thought and Taoism Mary Evelyn Tucker.

The universe story has been studied and taught in many places around the world in the years since, especially by religious women, the prophetic wing of the Church. I joined with other colleagues and friends to design graduate programs that reflected the magnitude of Thomas's work and vision. On that fateful afternoon, however, I was unaware that what I was hearing marked a significant beginning to what I and many others now celebrate was his great work.

JIM CONLON

The Universe Story:
Our Quest for Authentic Spiritual Experience

A turning point in the spiritual experience of the people that is as significant as the one that occurred at the birth of the new religions such as Judaism, Christianity, and Islam is taking place today:

As I reflect on the causes and consequences of this present moment, I focus my attention on what the American experience has uncovered. I ponder the values and practice of our spirituality today.

A functional spirituality for our time can be understood in and through the universe story. The impact of the universe story is similar to the impact of the great religions. We live in a great transitional moment when the emphasis on science as an abstract mechanism has left us bereft of a cosmology. Today we must understand the significance of technology for our world as well as its devastating impact on the Earth itself.

We need an adequate cosmic/human context to respond to the needs of our time. We need to reconsider the following:

- The idea that divine is transcends the natural world. This opposes the notion of the natural world as the locus of the meeting of the divine and the human.
- The idea that the human transcends the natural world. The result of this is that we simply see nature as an external object. This opposes the view that the universe is a communion of subject and not a collection of objects.
- The idea of a millennial bliss to be attain through the redemptive order (fall/redemption).

- The idea that it is not possible to achieve fulfillment without ever-increased consumption.
- The emphasis on salvation dynamics, at the expense of creation dynamics. This gives license to the freedom to destroy nature.
- The emergence of pietistic practices and a lack of moral discipline.

What is needed is a dynamic integration of the human/cosmic process. The result will be an activation of that which is necessary for life to flourish on Earth. The human psyche has self-evolved to understand the fourfold cosmic sequence: the emergence of the galactic system, the formation of planet Earth, the emergence of life, the emergence of human consciousness.

And its deepest level, human consciousness has awareness of divine presence. Today we are in the midst of creating a spirituality for the ecological age. For the first time in history, the human community has a single cosmic story. The result is the emergence of a functional cosmology that was unavailable throughout history.

The shift from a machine metaphor (Descartes, Newton) to a vital organic metaphor will result in new cultural coding that we can call an *ecological functional cosmology*. This is the most vital event taking place throughout the world in the context of the future well-being of the planet and the birth of creation-centered spirituality. A new vigor is now available for Christianity by reflecting on the organic development of the universe.

Jim Conlon

The Call to the True Self

Thomas Merton was a person of curiosity and courage. Describing a most powerful moment of prayer, he wrote, "I think for the first time in my whole life I really began to pray—praying not with my whole life with my lips and with my intellect and my imagination, but praying out the very roots of my life and of my being, and praying to the God I had never known."

Merton wrote with deep clarity about the immediacy of his personal experience, in a way that was true in his time and remains true to us today. His writings addressed many themes, including personal conversion; mysticism; and issues of war, peace, and civil rights. He was an artist, poet, writer, and photographer, and his vision was free of any tendency toward sentimentality. He was inspired by the work of Bernard of Clairvaux, who wrote, "You will find something more in woods than in books. Trees and stones will teach you that which you can never learn from masters."

Merton awakened us to the beauty of the natural world. His creative spirit was nourished by the words of Hildegard of Bingen, who wrote, "The person who does good works is indeed this orchard *bearing* good *fruit.*"

Thomas Merton's enduring appeal comes from his reflection on the call of the true self. He challenges us to be people of an open heart and mind, and encourages us to have an undefended intimate encounter with the divine.

Richard Rohr picks up on this theme in *The Naked Now*, where he writes about the call for the authentic self, undefended and open before God. He invites us to respond to Merton's invitation to become our true self, naked before the divine, and untouched by illusion. He urges us to take down the shield of the heart and allow the divine to see us as we truly are. When we are able to do this, we discover that the divine we seek has been there all the time.

Merton embraced the natural world as a source of divine presence. He writes, "The silence of the forest is my bride and the sweet dark warmth of the whole world is my love, and out of the heart of that dark warmth, comes the secret that is heard only in silence." He invites to remain in solitude long enough to emerge as the person we are meant to be.

When we plunge into the deep interiority of our soul, we discover there, beyond any inordinate self-consciousness, the wellspring we dare to call our life.

Jim Conlon

Poetry: A Dream on Paper

Poetry has been a vehicle for me to reach what lies deep within and to express it without becoming entangled in too much rational thought. The psyche is able to transcend the abstract left brain while capturing the great gift of human language that originates in the imagistic, holistic right brain.

Poetry affords the opportunity to have a dialogue with the pad of paper. The paper serves as a dialogical partner, a spiritual companion, whose empty page is the willing recipient of whatever lies in my heart and longs to be heard.

Sometimes I think of poetry as a dream on paper—a way to translate the impulses of the soul into shareable forms.

Poetry gives expression to blessings, to intuitive images that hover in the human sacred, beyond the embrace of ordinary conscious thought. Poetry is the midwife of those sacred impulses that emerge from another world, the land of the preconscious.

Poetry is prayer. Words arise from the inmost self and emerge unbidden from it, as an incense of hope and inspiration for the invisible incarnate one.

Poetry is a heart language that can give expression to the cosmos, where hidden hopes and aspirations lie.

Poems are the manifestations of a marinated soul. They offer a birth canal where unborn articulations of life's great mysteries emerge into the conscious world to reveal past journeys and predict future paths.

The poem is an oracle, a golden thread that makes visible for a passing moment a road map of our destiny through another mode of understanding.

There is so much to ponder, and so many doorways of surprise. Touch the mystery, bow in humble admiration to the words that come from another place and find expression on the landscape of Earth.

All is welcome now, everyone is present: the turtle and the polliwog, the poem and the person. Each is a lyric of life, a declaration of inspiration and hope.

Poetry is the art form of the mystics, the clarion call of the prophet.

Poetic words originate from another place; they tell of truths and narratives not yet understood.

Poems are canaries; they tell of safety and peril.

Poems are songs of yesterday and tomorrow announced today.

Poems pay attention to what our world has overlooked; they speak of other worlds and take us to a new time and space and understanding.

Poems announce the morning and bid farewell to night. They discover divinity in surprising places—in books, cornfields, sleepless nights, sunshine and sorrow, and in creatures great and small.

When I write a poem, I gain insight into my personal life and the pathology and promise of the world around me. I feel the pain of death, so prevalent in my midst: death in the streets; death to the visions of youth and dreams of old; death in my heart; yes, even the possible death of Earth.

Yet in the midst of it all, I experience hope, and wonder why. Is there not hope in the hearts of many when a child is born?

There is hope when a flower bursts forth from a crack in a broken sidewalk. There is hope when night turns to day, winter to spring. And in the immeasurable moment we know from our tradition, death turns into life; we call this "resurrection."

Poems tell courageous tales of love and loss and hopes not yet realized.

Poems are proclamations of amazement. They are always accompanied by beyondness, yet fully immersed in the mud and waters of life.

Prayer: An Encounter with Mystery

Prayer once puzzled me, particularly the prayer of petition. "Is prayer a way to change God's mind?" I wondered. I prayed for my mother when she had cancer, but she didn't get well. Was my prayer answered? Did God say no? My catechism said that prayer was "the elevation of the heart and mind to God." What did that mean?

Later I began to understand that prayer was more about gratitude and praise than about "give me and forgive me." It was not about changing God's mind, but rather about changing my mind about God.

Today I believe prayer is largely about conscious self-awareness, about paying attention to the divine that is already present. In fact, prayer is more about listening and responding than about formulating words. It opens us to epiphany moments in every aspect of our life and throughout all creation.

Prayer happens in silence and solitude as well as in the events of our everyday lives.

Prayer enhances our awareness of "God's action in the world." Prayer can be understood as reading the news of the day; I recall that a friend told me he would read the newspaper each day "to see what God was up to."

Prayer is not a script, nor a resuscitation of prepared words. Through prayer we become consciously aware that our lives are enveloped in the divine presence. Our tradition advises us to "pray always," and in this way to remain aware that each day, moment by moment, we are bathed in God.

Prayer is embracing the dynamics of an evolving universe.

Prayer happens when we bring into consciousness the original flaring forth of the universe, the formation of the galaxies and planets, followed by the emergence of life and the human.

Prayer allows us to awaken to who we are and to live our story more fully each day.

Prayer infuses us with the energy needed to live with depth, hope, inspiration and purpose.

Prayer is an opportunity to acknowledge our membership in the community of creation, to live reflectively with Earth. It is more about being than doing, more about presence than petition, more about wonder and awe than redemption. Teilhard de Chardin counsels us to spend more time on creation and less on redemption.

Mary Oliver reminds us that prayer comes from noticing; it is an act of intimacy with all we encounter.

Meister Eckhart says, "If the only prayer you said in your whole life was 'thank you,' that would suffice."

He also asserts that if he spends enough time with a caterpillar, he will never have to prepare another sermon; in other words, every expression of creation is "soaked in God," permeated with divine presence.

Prayer is being with God in our journey through life. It means entering into the important moments in our life and the lives of others.

Prayer is embracing the dynamics of an evolving universe.

Prayer is living with spontaneity and compassion.

Prayer happens when we gaze at the beauty of the night sky or the bluebird caroling from a tree, as we search for language and symbols to express the inexpressible.

Prayer may be contemplating a sunset. It may be reflecting on the issues of life: birth, love, work, wonder and death.

Prayer is gratitude and acknowledgment.

Prayer is the deepest desire of our life, through which the divine is revealed in our midst.

Prayer is a conversation, a shared burden, a celebration of excitement.

Prayer means living in the soft embrace of divine energy that enfolds our presence and heals our pain. It is an opportunity to renew our deep-seated desire for a life of justice, peace, and renewed possibilities.

Prayer is paying attention to the breath of life, to the reality of doubt, to what could be.

Prayer is paradox. In unexpected moments when insight comes, stillness happens and we feel bathed in God. Prayer happens in turbulence and also in a quiet moment when we listen to an unfamiliar voice that offers guidance for the way ahead in the ever-present now.

Prayer is an encounter with mystery. It can happen everywhere and always; it is an approach and attitude, an awareness that "God is in all things and all things are in God."

Spiritual Practice: Habits of the Heart

Growing up in rural Southern Ontario, the family rosary was a practice insisted on by my father. It reminded me of who I was, although I often migrated to the softest chair on which to kneel. Now I look back on it with gratitude.

Other events in my early years indelibly imprinted on me the importance of spiritual practice. The Stations of the Cross was conducted weekly during Lent, led by the priest and myself as an altar boy. We recited prayers before each station numbered from Jesus' condemnation to death to his crucifixion and resurrection. There were also novenas, prayers to Mary, the mother of Jesus, for special assistance during challenging times in our lives. This was referred to as the Novena of Our Mother of Perpetual Help.

Other kinds of practices influenced me in my growing years. I watched ballplayers and boxers make the sign of the cross before going to bat or beginning a prizefight. My father planted potatoes on St. Patrick's Day each year, with the hope they would nourish us and compensate for the famine that had left our ancestors on the brink of death.

Spiritual practice can be understood as a response to these questions: How do you deepen and enhance your spiritual journey? What practices keep you in touch with the sacred dimensions, move you beyond what Alan Watts calls the "skin-encapsulated ego" and connect you to a wider vision of the world where you experience mystery amidst the ordinary?

For some, spiritual practice means spending time with the natural world—the ocean, mountains, rocks and trees. For others, it means consciously embracing the dawn and dusk of each day. Yet others may visit an art gallery, listen to music or read the words from a sacred text or a favorite author.

Spiritual practice can be a repetitive act, such as repeating the rosary or a mantra. The repetitive practice of reciting prayers can move our awareness to life's great mysteries.

In essence, spiritual practice is our way of discovering the movement of the spirit through a dialogue with everyday life. In our practice, we acknowledge what we love and become empowered to act accordingly.

Our tradition counsels us to pray always. To do so is to collapse all separateness between the sacred and the secular.

The wisdom teacher Sheng-yen advises us in our spiritual practice with these words: "Be soft in your practice.... Follow the stream, have faith in its course. It will go its own way meandering here, trickling there. It will find the grooves, the cracks, the crevices. Just follow it. Never let it out of your sight. It will take you."

Thomas Moore writes of spiritual practice with these words: "All we have to do is live this life with openness, imagination and a sense of paradox and wonder... Only by seeing through to the eternal and blissful soul of our neighbor will we catch a glimpse of the unnamable."

Thomas Merton, author, monk and scholar of the spiritual life, spent much of his life encouraging people to engage in spiritual practice or prayer; however, he never at any time told people how to pray. With this in mind, we can suggest that spiritual practice is how each of us discovers how to pray. The following are some of the ways people have engaged in the practice.

Geo-justice

Cultural movements, like waves upon the shore of life, rise and fall, only to rise again. We have arrived at a time that is unique in the intensity of its challenge. It is a time to witness the melting away of static beliefs, and reconcile our experience of contemporary culture with our understanding of the revealed word of our Christian faith. It is a time to affirm our notion of God as holy mystery, to experience the divine presence while we become fully engaged in the great dramas of ecological devastation and human poverty. It is a time when a new wave of engagement calls us into action.

I call this movement *geo-justice*.

Geo-justice is a vision that brings the human, the Earth, the universe, and the divine into a profound immediacy with each other. It is a process to re-imagine the world as we would like it to be, and to take concrete steps to make that possible. Geo-justice is a journey that takes us to the far reaches of the universe and returns us to each new moment, in which we become agents of transformation.

Myths bring energy to people, shaping their perceptions, unifying their vision. To undo our present ecological devastation, we need a new myth. Geo-justice is an operative myth for our time.

Geo-justice is a preferential option promising justice for the whole Earth and its people. In this perspective, no significant decision or action occurs without assessing how that action or decision would affect the Earth. As we move toward this preferential option, we can draw upon the theological paradigms from the past and rediscover and reinvigorate their meaning.

Integral Ecology

Thomas Berry's often quoted phrase "the universe is a communion of subjects, not a collection of objects" speaks directly to his vision of an integral ecology. In this statement, he emphasizes how we exist in relationship with the Earth, as people of the Earth, and stresses the depths and interconnection in all our relationships. This spiritual-physical communion can be understood as foundational for integral ecology. Berry writes, "The integral ecologist can now be considered a normative guide for our times.... The integral ecologist is the spokesperson for the planet."

In *The Cry of the Earth, the Cry of the Poor,* Leonardo Boff unites his concern for those overwhelmed by poverty in the barrios of Brazil with his concern for the parched, arid lands of his home country. The first to use the term *integral ecology* in print, he writes about the need to connect our spiritual vision with the needs of the people and the planet.

I see the work of Berry and Boff as foundational to the vision of integral ecology named by Pope Francis in his letter to the world, *Laudato Si'*. In this encyclical, he writes, "We are faced not with two separate crises, one environmental and the other social, but rather with one complex crisis which is both social and environmental." And he says, "A true ecological approach always becomes a social approach... so as to hear both the cry of the Earth and the cry of the poor."

Integral ecology implies a departure from the prior emphasis on social over ecological concerns and instills a new relationship between society and nature that will result in the preservation of life as we know it. This is an issue we can no longer ignore. Integral ecology must serve as our gospel of the moment.

Transgenetic Cosmology

I stand in awe of and admiration for those who have preceded me on the journey. Based on experience, friendship, and reflection, I wish to bring forward a renewed and fresh approach that will make possible a praxis.

From this deep and abiding journey, I strive to create a dynamic synthesis of science (evolution) and art (creativity imagination) and mysticism (an experience that invigorates a world a balance, harmony, and peace). I propose that, through science, we are able to embrace the reality of evolution and discover and experience that which is always awakening us to what is up ahead. As people of transformation and change, we can create a world that is different and transformed.

I have taken Thomas Berry's term of "transgenetic cultural coding" and created a new term for this journey, which I like to call *transgenetic cosmology*.

I see a transgenetic cosmology as the source of vision, transformation, and change. It is the force behind our capacity for a second birth.

We celebrate and transform the tendencies that rise up in our imagination. From that place, we evoke, express, and empower ourselves to move forward and achieve marvelous things.

The question I ponder is "How do we alter our perception of the world so it incorporates the wisdom of science, art, and mysticism?"

I believe that only when we are freed of the obstacles that stand in the way of wonder, beauty, and surprise can we respond to the emerging dynamics of the world into which we are born.

It occurs to me that a transgenetic cosmology involves both listening and strategic engagement in appropriate and necessary action. The process includes the following:

- Retrieve memories of childhood encounters with beauty and wonder in the natural world
- Recollect stories that are personal, cultural, and traditional
- Create art that expresses the sacred impulse imbedded in the soul

The Edge of Our Longing

As we stand here at the edge of our longing, positioned at the threshold of sacredness and depth, images of tomorrow emerge into consciousness bringing a new vision of hope to a world immersed in anxiety.

Hope from a new vision of monastery whose architecture is created out of the dynamic relationships that are nurtured by the wonder of the universe and our place in the future.

Hope from a fresh vision of novitiate, where each person's cosmological imagination reveals what it means to be human in an unfolding universe.

Hope from a renewed sense of home, an experience whereby we are re-energized to heal the wound of homelessness, and become energized for the journey, like a horse who enthusiastically gallops when pointed toward home.

Hope from a gallery of beauty that touches every soul and reminds us of the gorgeous planet that invites us to commune and be at one.

Within this galaxy of images resides a unity, a healing oneness that unites point zero and ground zero, the crack in the ozone layer and the crack in the street, and all that is a manifestation of beauty to heal our longing for sacredness and depth.

Jim Conlon

From the Stars to the Street

As we experience radical amazement at the wonder of the universe and extend compassionate action to the poor and suffering, the least, the lost, and the left behind, we awaken to a new opportunity. Our response will be prompted by an enhanced sensitivity that extends to self, other, Earth, and God. It will be signified by widening compassion as we respond to the needs and desires of all members of our planetary community.

Through contemplation, liberation, and creation-centered engagements, we will witness the unlocked power of each person, connect the stars to the streets, and inaugurate the work of engaged cosmology.

In this new historical moment, we confront injustice and discover a new meaning of grace through the experience and practice of fairness, fulfillment, freedom, community, and unconditional love. Our experience of grace will offer fresh understanding of each benevolent moment and each person whose unconditional love permeates all of life and all creation.

The capacity to transcend social isolation and patterns of separation will increase the experience of acceptance and belonging. It will move us to appreciation and solidarity, supported by gestures of deep listening and recognition. In our spiritual practice we will discover a new sense of community and fulfillment, a new experience of mutuality, love, and an increased capacity for vulnerability.

The experience of support, newfound friendships, and belonging will strengthen our work and provide increased purpose and meaning to our lives. From this new place, we will collectively build an agenda for the future that is energized and practiced within a web of genuine engagement expressed as a balance of vision and action. Our new engagement will heal the degradation of abusive power while it inspires courage, creativity, and hope; in circles of solidarity, we can imagine a better future and, as civil rights activist/historian W. E. B. Dubois phrased it, "respond to the mighty causes that call us." Through the practice of engaged cosmology, we participate in acts of service and justice at an unprecedented level; our engagements bring out the best in us and connect our actions to our hearts. We realize that what needs to be healed is our sense of separation. We locate ourselves within this universe and discover a world of love, kindness, and caring that transforms fear and despair into trust and hope.

Through the practice and appreciation of contemplation, liberation, and creation, we establish an integral and inclusive presence that is open to the divine and committed to a life of service and compassion. Increased trust and solidarity will heal and transform our cynicism and turn boredom into radical amazement and into a life of engagement and spiritual practice.

Each person's narrative of engagement will embrace faith and be transformed in a new world of love and social solidarity. People of engaged cosmology, uniting the stars to the streets, will address the concrete circumstances of life with expanded consciousness and a new sense of the sacred, viewing everyone as a member of a beloved community nourished by a fresh and universal and inclusive spirituality.

Jim Conlon

Pondering on the Precipice

As the world continues to churn with ripples of unrest, we pursue a new moment of solitude as we peer over the precipice of wonder and gaze into the mystery before us. Mystery envelops our awareness of society and soul and encompasses the sacred planet in this new moment of grace, as the divine presence continues to unfold. We allow our imagination to soar and to embrace the beauty of creation, even amidst the poverty and devastation that reside across the world these days.

We pray today that from the depths of our society, planet, and soul, we may be anointed with a healing bond of freedom that will touch the world with wonder, mystery, and surprise. Emerging from this new moment, we venture forth into each galactic opportunity to experience the depth of the incarnation, to wonder as "the flesh becomes word" and flares forth into an as-yet-unimagined life.

With each new awareness, we remember how life burst forth on this planet and gave birth to the untrodden path that it is now our challenge to walk. As we move toward accomplishing the next steps on our journey, we compose the beatitudes of the new creation that dares to await us and calls us forth into an era of grateful peace.

We hear the call today. It is a cry for fresh energy and zest for life, in a moment of aliveness and a moment of grace. As we cocreate a wondrous future to heal the Earth and nourish new life, we listen attentively with gratitude and joy to the longings of creation. We venture forth into a time of prolonged engagement, when our dreams will emerge from the deep wells of wisdom. We imagine a new era that will refresh our souls and renew the face of the Earth.

As beauty bursts forth, we feel the joyful and tender embrace of soul, life, and Earth, enveloped in the sacred, pulsating presence of our God. This presence will heal all our longings and quench our thirst for sacredness. As we announce the great "I am" of the gospel that pulsates through each of our days, we long to tell the story of how things began. The sacred breakthrough moments of creation, liberation, and contemplation bubble up from our hearts and invite us toward fresh engagement. On our journey, the Spirit speaks to us at the edge of wonder as we gaze into the mystery of our emerging, viable, and energized future.

Becoming Planetary People

We stand on the precipice of new beginnings and ponder the constant and enduring question, and ask, "What is possible and necessary for us to do at this time in human/Earth history?"

Drawing on the wisdom that echoes from the past and irrigates our soul, we move forward. We bring programs and projects of personal and social transformation to the planetary people who await us. This is a journey we must make together; it is a journey we take with our hearts ajar. On it, we honor and celebrate each unique gift that we long to bring forth to the world—gifts of images, lyrics, courage, justice making, beauty, and sound.

As a newly fashioned planetary people, we co-create circles of inclusiveness and compassion. Each step along the way carries us forward in the footprints of the sacred; each moment, we are enveloped in the embrace of an evolving, unfinished universe. We locate our mysterious journey within the great unfolding, fourteen-billion-year story of the universe. Together, we respond with fresh energy to the invitation to make our contribution to advance the unfinished mystery that defines our work as a planetary people.

A New Morning

It's morning again.
Sister Sun peeks over the hemlocks.
Brother Moon disappears into the far-off sky.
Now is our time.

I listen to the fractures
of my broken heart,
yet I pray that cosmic beauty
may thrive again
at the dawn of this new time.

Epilogue: What You Dare to Call Your Life

Feel the fresh breeze on your face. You were born for this time.

Yes, you were chosen to walk upon Springbank's green earth. Feel the energy, the infusion of divine, creative love—the dabar of life that flows through each present moment.

I say a prayer of thanks that I am invited by the great mystery to live at this time.

As Thomas Berry would say, "you were chosen."

With all that's happening in this grace-filled moment, the Ancient One of days invites you to bask in the beauty of each untrodden path.

As we awaken into a new time of joy, peace, and happiness, we are invited here at Springbank to activate our participation in the creative arts, such as poetry, pottery, and painting, as we gratefully embrace and anticipate the days ahead.

We see life and the world no longer as a vestibule for heaven but rather as a place to let heaven happen now. We celebrate a renewed sense of sacredness and feel the immanent presence of the divine calling us into a new time, an era of love, beauty and amazement.

As you contemplate what is next, joyfully receive the sacred invitation to frolic among the trees, enjoying the companionship of Max, Jake, and Shelly. Savor the sunlight. Plunge into the wellspring that you and Teilhard dare to call your life.

Springbank Papers

About the Author

Jim Conlon was born in Canada in 1936. He received a degree in chemistry from Assumption University of Windsor, and later in theology from the University of Western Ontario, and a PhD from Union Institute and Graduate School. Deeply moved by the impact of the second Vatican Council, the civil rights movement, and the Vietnam War, Jim moved from pastoral work to the streets. Today he is one of the leading teachers of the new narrative of the cosmos.

For more information and a complete list of Jim's published works, see: www.jimconlon.net.

Contact: Springbank: 843-372-6311 or springbank@springbankretreat.org

www.ingramcontent.com/pod-product-compliance
Lightning Source LLC
Chambersburg PA
CBHW040419100526
44589CB00021B/2762